Parables of Matthew

Daniel J. Davis, Sr.

faithQuest® ◆ Brethren Press®

Covenant Bible Studies Series

Unless otherwise noted, scripture quotations are from the New Revised Standard Version of the Bible, copyrighted 1989 by the National Council of Churches of Christ in the USA, Division of Education and Ministry.

Cover photo: D. Jeanene Tiner

02 01 00 99 98   5 4 3 2 1

Library of Congress Catalog Card No. 98-074304

Manufactured in the United States of America

Contents

Foreword

The Covenant Bible Studies Series was first developed for a denominational program in the Church of the Brethren and the Christian Church (Disciples of Christ). This program, called People of the Covenant, was founded on the concept of relational Bible study and has been adopted by several other denominations and small groups who want to study the Bible in a community rather than alone.

Relational Bible study is marked by certain characteristics, some of which differ from other types of Bible study. For one, it is intended for small groups of people who can meet face-to-face on a regular basis and share frankly with an intimate group. It is important to remember that relational Bible study is anchored in covenantal history. God covenanted with people in Old Testament history, established a new covenant in Jesus Christ, and covenants with the church today.

Relational Bible study takes seriously a corporate faith. As each person contributes to study, prayer, and work, the group becomes the real body of Christ. Each one's contribution is needed and important. "For just as the body is one and has many members, and all the members of the body, though many, are one body, so it is with Christ. . . . Now you are the body of Christ and individually members of it" (1 Cor. 12:12,17).

Relational Bible study helps both individuals and the group to claim the promise of the Spirit and the working of the Spirit. As one person testified, "In our commitment to one another and in our sharing, something happened. . . . We were woven together in love by the Master Weaver. It is something that can happen only when two or three or seven are gathered in God's name, and we know the promise of God's presence in our lives."

For people who choose to use this study in a small group, the following guidelines will help create an atmosphere in which support will grow and faith will deepen.

1. As a small group of learners, we gather around God's word to discern its meaning for today.
2. The words, stories, and admonitions we find in scripture come alive for today, challenging and renewing us.
3. All people are learners and all are leaders.
4. Each person will contribute to the study, sharing the meaning found in the scripture and helping to bring meaning to others.
5. We recognize each other's vulnerability as we share out of our own experience, and in sharing we learn to trust others and to be trustworthy.

Additional suggestions for study and group-building are provided in the "Sharing and Prayer" section. They are intended for use in the hour preceding the Bible study to foster intimacy in the covenant group and relate personal sharing to the Bible study topic.

Welcome to this study. As you search the scriptures, may you also search yourself. May God's voice and guidance and the love and encouragement of brothers and sisters in Christ challenge you to live more fully the abundant life God promises.

Resources for This Study

Bruner, Frederick Dale. *Matthew, A Commentary, Vol. 2* (The Churchbook: Matthew 13–28). Word, 1990.

Crossan, John Dominic. *In Parables,* rev. ed. Polebridge Press, 1992.

_____. *Jesus: A Revolutionary Biography.* Harper and Row, 1995.

Gardner, Richard B. *Matthew* (Believers Church Bible Commentary). Herald Press, 1991.

Hare, Douglas R. A. *Matthew* (Interpretation Series). John Knox Press, 1993.

Mays, James L., ed. *Harper's Bible Commentary.* Harper and Row, 1988.

Via, Dan Otto, Jr. *The Parables.* Fortress Press, 1967.

Preface

Parable. It's a common word and a common idea among Christians. But when you really begin to look at the teaching stories of Jesus, parable becomes what I call a "red cap" word. Remember when trains ran across the country? At every station porters, called Red Caps because of their red hats, carried your baggage. Well, a "red cap" word carries a lot of baggage.

What do these peculiar little stories mean? One important key to understanding the parables is understanding what Matthew's Gospel as a whole is all about. In a nutshell, the Gospel reflects the birth and growth of the new church community. Matthew shows how Jesus carved the Christian movement right out of Jewish tradition, sometimes embracing the traditional ways, sometimes debating Pharisaic Judaism. Matthew was never over against Judaism. In fact, he was a Jew himself, but he was also a passionate advocate for the growing Christian movement. Jesus, from Matthew's point of view, made his way brilliantly between tradition and blessing.

Matthew's Gospel is first in the canon because it is "the church's book." His overarching concern is to organize believing Christians into a community with rules and procedures, teachings and doctrines, prayers and processes. Jesus did not return as soon as Mark had expected, judging from the urgency in his Gospel, so Matthew and his readers were beginning to think that the kingdom was both already here and not yet here. With the second coming still in the future, Matthew's community had time to preserve the stories, build the tradition, and organize what became the church.

Writing ten or more years after Mark, Matthew could extend his narrative both backward through the generations and forward to the end of the age. He begins the account with a backward look at the genealogy of Jesus Christ and ends looking forward, transferring authority and responsibility to Jesus and, by extension, to the ongoing and organized community of believers: "All authority in heaven and on earth has been given to me. Go therefore and make disciples of all nations, baptizing them in the name of the Father and of the Son and of the Holy Spirit, and teaching them to obey everything that I have commanded you. And remember, I am with you always, to the end of the age" (Matt. 28:18-20).

—Daniel J. Davis, Sr.

1

The Mustard Seed
Matthew 13:31-32, 34-35

*Though sometimes shocking and sometimes not what
we want to hear, the parables express some of the most
difficult concepts to understand: the kingdom of God,
relationships to God and to each other, judgment and
grace, the end times.*

Personal Preparation

1. Memorize Matthew 13:31-32, the parable of the Mustard Seed. What does this parable mean to you? Jot a few
   ideas in the margins. Bring your ideas to the group.
2. Consider your own understanding of God, the kingdom,
   and judgment. Why do you think Jesus spoke about these
   things in parables? Why wouldn't Jesus come straight
   out and tell what they mean? When have you used
   parables to teach children? Why do you or don't you come
   straight out with information for young children?
3. A parable like the parable of the Laborers in the Vineyard (Matt. 20:1-16) completely undoes some of our no-
   tions of what is fair or just. In your own faith, which of
   your former ideas or beliefs have been undone or ex-
   ploded? What about your faith has been comforting? What
   has been shattering?
4. Try thinking in parables this week. Tell who God is or
   what the kingdom is all about by completing the sentence "The kingdom of God is like . . ." or "God is like . . ."

Also try thinking in parables about other difficult concepts, such as the Holy Spirit, the resurrection, salvation, and faith. Bring your parables to the group.

Understanding

I had a supervisor one time who liked to recite little anecdotes from his experiences. Then he'd say, "Gosh, that's a parable!" Most of the time, however, his little parables were merely nice illustrations of a point he was trying to make; but every once in a while, when I least expected it, his little story would skewer me, hitting me right where I lived.

Once he told the story about the minister who was traveling through an airport and bought half a dozen gourmet chocolate chip cookies for the trip home. He sat down to wait for the plane, and about a minute later he noticed the woman next to him reach over and take a cookie out of the bag. Well okay, he thought. Then he reached over and took a cookie. She looked at him a bit funny but didn't say anything. And so it went until the six cookies were gone. Neither said anything to the other, of course. Soon he boarded his plane. As he sat in his seat thinking about the incident, he opened his briefcase, and, to his great embarrassment, he found his bag of six chocolate chip cookies.

This story may not be a parable in the fashion of Jesus, but it illustrates some of the characteristics of a biblical parable. It has an unexpected twist—the conventional order of things gets turned around. And the story helps the hearer understand a concept, such as true generosity or hospitality.

More than that, however, parables are unsettling stories. Most of us tend to think of them as pithy nuggets of truth—and they are—but, as Jesus used them, they're also dangerous. They draw us in. They ask us to identify with them. Then they convict us! Ultimately, though, after they convict us, they enlighten those with ears to hear and eyes to see.

Parables turn the world upside down. When Jesus preaches in Matthew, he reorders conventional wisdom. You must endure abuse instead of retaliating against your abusers; you must love your enemies instead of hating them; and you must forgive those who offend you instead of punishing them. But Jesus' preaching reaches the level of personal revelation when Jesus says these same things in the form of a parable. For instance, the parable of the Unforgiving Servant (Matt. 18:23-35) jolts us, upending our former way of seeing it, and gives us a new way to see what suddenly seems absolutely right.

The parables are deceptively simple, like the little William Carlos Williams poem about the red wheelbarrow. The four-line poem presents a vivid image of a red wheelbarrow and white chickens. This image calls forth, at least for me, all kinds of memories and associations from childhood, including the red wheelbarrow my grandfather gave me. As the poet says, so much depends on a simple image. It's like that with parables. The briefest parable, like the Parable of the Mustard Seed, is full of meaning in its simplicity.

What a Parable Is

Typically, Jesus taught and preached using parables. Over a third of the first three Gospels is parable. Most of them are brief; some are just a single sentence long. Most seem to apply to particular situations of Jesus' day, though some are more general. Many use ordinary, everyday images or settings. Most challenge the things we routinely take for granted.

The parables express some of the most difficult concepts for the mind to understand. In Matthew they describe the kingdom of God, relationships to God and to each other, judgment and grace, and the end times. How would we describe these things, given the chance? No way has proved better than the parable, if we listen with our hearts as well as our minds.

In some ways it's hard to say what a parable is. Is it a riddle? a fable with a moral? an illustration? While parables have touched us deeply and helped us to understand much, we have always had trouble defining them. According to Bible historian Robert Grant, the church in the Middle Ages had a little poem to help people learn the different types of literature in the Bible. It goes like this:

The letter shows us what God and our fathers did;
   Littera gesta docet,
The allegory shows us where our faith is hid;
   quid credo allegoria,
The moral meaning gives us rules of daily life;
   Moralis quid agas,
The anagogy shows us where we end our strife.
   quo tendas anagogia.

Anagogy is the spiritual or heavenly meaning of scripture. Yet even here parable defies categorization.

John Dominic Crossan, probably the most gifted interpreter of parable, describes parable in his book *In Parables* as expressing something that cannot be expressed in any other way. What's more, a parable invites us to participate in the reality it expresses. That is, a parable invites us "in," as Crossan would say. If it is expressing grace, it invites us to experience grace. If it tells who God is, it invites us to know God more intimately. But we can't just "domesticate" the parables of Jesus, like a comfortable old cat that cuddles up in our lap. The parables keep surprising us. Just when we think we've got one figured out, just when we're ready to participate in its truth at one level, it slips away to another level.

Even Crossan, for all his gifts as a writer and storyteller, never really "defines" parable. The dictionary isn't much help either, because any definitions it offers are always a matter of "yes, but." Yes, it is a story with moral importance, but it is not a moral. Yes, it uses some allegory, but it is not strictly allegorical. Perhaps it would be much easier to say what a parable is not than to say what it is.

Parable sometimes illustrates a moral or spiritual truth, as with the parable of the Unforgiving Servant, but more often, a parable *is* a moral or spiritual truth. Parable can't be reduced to a fable, like Aesop told. It's usually difficult to say "and the moral of the story is . . ." Neither can parable be reduced to an allegory, as in *Pilgrim's Progress* where "this" equals "that." Often the parable has a point. Many times it has several points, and occasionally it leaves you without a point at all. It's a story.

Telling Stories

We listen to stories with more attention than any other kind of speech. It's not surprising that storytelling is a feature of probably every culture in the world. Stories hook us. They contain the very meaning of human life. They help us make sense of the world. We use them to express our feelings. We use them to help others understand what we mean. And the stories we tell help us to understand ourselves in ways so deep we can't do it any other way.

Here is a story about a story. "Plant a radish, get a radish—not a brussel sprout. That's why I like veg'tables, you know what they're about!" Two neighboring fathers in the musical *The Fantasticks* struggle with their kids, a boy and a girl. They alternately hope (and conspire) to marry their children to each other and grouse at each other. Both are bewildered by the crazy things their kids do. Why, those kids just don't get it, claims one father as he sings to the other about his garden. At least vegetables are predictable. The doggone kids just aren't. Can't you just picture Walter Matthau and Jack Lemmon doing this scene? Well, of course, it turns out that the garden isn't all that much more predictable than the kids, and the fathers are probably more unpredictable than they think their kids are.

Jesus tells a little story about a mustard seed, a thing with a certain degree of predictability in Jesus' day. Yet the mustard seed (not *really* the smallest of all seeds, but who cares) grows and becomes something we wouldn't expect—a shrub so big that it's a tree filled with birds' nests. "The kingdom of heaven is like a mustard seed that someone took and sowed in his field; it is the smallest of all the seeds, but when it is has grown, it is the greatest of shrubs and becomes a tree; so that birds of the air come and make nests in its branches" (Matt. 13:31-32).

It's too easy to interpret this little parable as a parable of growth, i.e., the more you grow in faith, the more magnificent you will become. Most likely, the parable describes the realm of heaven. In the realm of heaven things are not what we expect. In the kingdom of heaven, what we see is not what we get. Or maybe, what we get is not what we see. This is not really a parable of becoming (growth) so much as it is a parable of coming (the advent of the kingdom)—and it will not be what we think it is supposed to be.

Matthew's Plan

In some ways, Matthew's is the most well organized of the four New Testament Gospels. It consists of an alternating pattern of narrative (story) and discourse, five sets of each. A narrative tells us what Jesus was doing, and a discourse tells us what Jesus was saying. Each narrative is characterized by "fulfillment quotations" (e.g., 1:22) and each discourse ends with a "formula quotation" (e.g., Matt. 7:28; 11:1; 13:53; 19:1; 26:1).

The first narrative section describes the advent, birth, and early ministry of Jesus. It is followed by the Sermon on the Mount, a discourse that roughly parallels the giving of the law on Mount Sinai to Moses. The second narrative section tells of the miracles of Jesus, a group of ten stories in chapters 8 and 9. It is followed by a "missionary discourse" (Matt. 10:5-42). The third narrative deals with the story of growing opposition to Jesus' ministry from the scribes and Pharisees." This third narrative is followed by a discourse on the coming of the realm of God, which contains a major collection of parables (Matt. 13).

The fourth narrative tells stories of Jesus' ministry, particularly the death of John the Baptizer, the feeding of the 5000, walking on water, healings at Gennesaret, more struggles with the religious leadership, and the like. This section also includes the stories that foretell Jesus' passion and the transfiguration. Then the discourse that follows in chapter 18 centers on regulations for the life of the new community who will carry on Jesus' ministry and includes parables of relationship (the parables of the Lost Sheep and the Unforgiving Servant).

The fifth narrative is the story of Jesus' journey to Jerusalem that precedes the passion story. The related discourse is in chapter 25 and is Matthew's version of the apocalyptic discourse (cf., Mark 13); it contains parable-like stories of the end times, such as the Ten Maidens, the Talents, and the Last Judgment. The concluding section of the Gospel is, of course, the passion and resurrection narrative, which ends with the Great Commission.

Between the birth and the resurrection stories, Matthew organizes his Gospel as a possible parallel to the five books of Moses, a new Torah for a new community of faith. Reaching back to call on the truth that was from the beginning with the ancients, Matthew points us forward to the fulfillment of everything that has been promised. The parables are the foretaste of what is now, but not yet.

A parable. An image that calls forth memories. A story that expresses an irreducible truth. A sack of gourmet cookies. A mustard seed. The kingdom of heaven.

Discussion and Action

1. As a group, take a stab at defining parable as a group. How did you do? Why do parables defy definition?
2. Read aloud some of the parables you wrote in preparation for the session. Discuss how others' parables surprised you, convicted you, informed you?
3. Walk through the Gospel of Matthew quickly, seeing where the narratives and discourses begin and end. Why do you think parables are an effective teaching method?
4. The parables in Matthew help us understand God, the kingdom, God's judgment, and the end times. Try to describe these things literally. What do you come up with? Are the descriptions accurate?
5. Read or say the parable of the Mustard Seed together aloud. How many different meanings do you see in this simple parable? Which, if any, is the "right" meaning?
6. If the realm of heaven is not what it seems, what is it that we have been expecting all along, and how do you think it will be different from our expectation?
7. Make a sun catcher to remind you of the mustard seed parable. Cut a hole in the bottom of a clear plastic beverage cup. Put a few mustard seeds in the cup. Place the cup right side up on a metal baking sheet and bake at 350 degrees for one to two minutes or until the plastic cup is melted. Take the cup from the oven and cool. Put a string

or yarn through the hole and hang it in a window. To
make a colored sun catcher, put crayon shavings about
an inch deep in the cup before baking.

8. Close by singing "Tell me the stories of Jesus."

2

Three Simple Parables: Yeast, Treasure, Pearl
Matthew 13:33-35, 44-46

Joy in the kingdom prompts us to give up all earthly treasure for the treasure of the kingdom.

Personal Preparation

1. Read Matthew 13:33-35. Start a collection of small, seemingly insignificant items this week that have the potential of becoming great, such as seed, pennies, yeast. Bring your collection to the group. Be prepared to say how these things are like the kingdom of God.

2. Read Matthew 13:44-46. What has given you the most joy in life? Did you have to give up anything to have this joy? Did you consider this a sacrifice? Why or why not?

3. Make a list of some of the simple truths by which you live your life. Look back at the list. Which ones are simple to say and simple to do? Which are simple to say and hard to do? Which ones have you carried off most successfully?

4. For a meditation this week, bake a loaf of bread from scratch, or use frozen roll dough, or dough in a cardboard tube in the refrigerated section of your grocery store. Keep track of the dough rising and meditate on how God makes great things from small things.

Understanding

You know the old saw that says the best things in life are free. Is that really true? Has it worked out that way for you in your life? One of the best things in my life has been reading, and it's free when I use the library. Reading is easy for me. I can't even remember a time when I couldn't read, and I surely don't remember learning. But is reading really free?

I suppose reading is free in the sense that it doesn't cost money, and in many ways reading is freeing. But reading sometimes costs a great deal. I've read things that have changed my life. I've seen myself in some of the things I've read, and it has made me want to change.

Things are never as simple as they seem. Perhaps we should even say, when you see a simple idea, watch out! There is likely to be some big explosion waiting to happen. If I were to rewrite the old saw, for instance, I'd say the best things in life come at a huge personal cost.

I think it was Ernest Hemingway who remarked that the best things in life aren't free. They're the most expensive things we'll ever learn. We learn them at great cost because we pay out our very lives learning them, in minutes and hours, days and years, over an entire lifetime. We literally pay for them with our lives.

Simple Parables . . .

The parable of the Yeast, the parable of the Hidden Treasure, and the parable of the Pearl of Great Value are not much longer than their titles. Each is only a sentence long; each is a simile or comparison; each is deceptively simple. All three parables begin with the same words: "the kingdom of heaven is like . . ." Then each fills in the blank: yeast, a treasure hidden in a field, a pearl of great value (a merchant in search of fine pearls). Simple enough.

At one level, these little parables use common ordinary images and mean what they say. We don't have to struggle to get the idea. Even those of us who buy Wonder Bread off the shelves in plastic bags know enough to recognize the reference to yeast. "Leaven" we might not get, but yeast is familiar enough. Who doesn't dream of finding a fortune somewhere. We're all greedy enough to dream about a lucrative real estate deal, especially if the land sits over an oil field. And I suppose most of us would be tempted to sell most of what we have for a pearl or a valuable painting or sculpture, especially if had greater value than all our other things put together.

But things are never as simple as they seem. It's not that the simple things are really hard. It's that the simple things are usually much richer in meaning than they appear on the surface.

Looking at these three parables in context will help us peel back one layer of their simultaneously simple and complex meanings. All three come from Matthew 13, which is one of the discourses that alternates with narratives throughout the Gospel. The narrative that precedes these parables tells about the growing opposition to Jesus' message: John the Baptist is arrested (Matt. 11) and Jesus tangles with the scribes and the Pharisees over the law. Thus, Jesus and his little band of followers draw in closer to withstand the persecution and begin to form what will become the church.

Then the parables that fill the discourse in Matthew 13 are stories depicting the church, foretold when Jesus named Simon Peter ("On this Rock I will build my church), and the fulfillment of the kingdom, about which he has been preaching.

Yeast

Jesus said, "The kingdom of heaven is like yeast that a woman took and mixed in with three measures of flour until all of it was leavened."

When I was in graduate school, I used to bake bread every Tuesday. At the time, we lived in a third-floor apartment with a transom over the door that opened onto a long hallway serving ten other apartments. Baking bread became a living parable for us.

I'd make the dough with flour and yeast. I'd knead it and punch it and roll it into a big ball. Then I'd put it in the old, chipped, crockery bowl that had belonged to my grandmother. I'd cover it with a dish towel and set it aside to rise while I read a book. After an hour or two, usually about 2 o'clock in the afternoon, I would divide the puffy dough among the pans and bake it.

At about 2:30 every Tuesday, Mike Ruddy needed to borrow a book. He lived down the hall, next to the elevator, and he too had a transom over his door. The smell of baking bread rising in the oven was just too much for him to resist. After three or four weeks, I just started putting an extra loaf in the oven.

The humble gospel of Jesus Christ is the irresistible yeast that attracts believers and makes the church grow into the living body of Christ. And in this church there is bread enough for everyone who believes.

Hidden Treasure

Jesus said, "The kingdom of heaven is like treasure hidden in a field, which someone found and hid; then in his joy he goes and sells all that he has and buys that field."

The Gospels tell us that we must sell everything and follow Jesus (Matt. 19:21; Mark 10:21; Luke 18:22), but this parable adds a motivation of joy here that we do not see elsewhere. In his commentary on Matthew, Bible scholar Dale Bruner notes that it is difficult to teach anything that people should do out of duty. It is far easier to teach them about joy and then watch them respond in obedience to the gospel. He points to the Ten Commandments, which begin with God's reminder to the people of why they should be joyful. "I am the Lord your God, who has brought you out of the land of Egypt, out of the house of bondage." "Then," Bruner says, "the commandments that follow are not joyless duties but joyful responses."

Selling all that we have is not a great sacrifice when the treasure is a joy to have. When I was in graduate school, my wife and I had an original Manet painting hanging in our living room. We lived in an old tenement apartment converted to married student housing on the south side of Chicago, and we had an original Manet! It cost us three dollars.

We didn't have to sell all that we had—which was nothing really—to have this treasure. In fact, the University of Chicago had a program funded by a generous gift to loan original works of great art to students for little or no money. What we had to do was wait in line overnight on the lawn, to choose the painting on a first-come-first-served basis. But who minded? It was worth even more than that to have this treasure in our home.

The Pearl of Great Value

Jesus said, "The kingdom of heaven is like a merchant in search of fine pearls; on finding one pearl of great value, he went and sold all that he had and bought it."

This parable is a twin to the parable of the Hidden Treasure. Both people joyfully sell all that they have to have something of even greater value. The parables of the yeast and the seed are also twins. They tell of something inconsequential that becomes great, but they are stories of how God is at work to make this happen. The two parables about treasure and pearls are about the human response to God's promise. Actors in the seed and yeast parables are a man and a woman. In the twin parables of the treasure and the pearl, the actors are poor and rich.

John Steinbeck also wrote a parable about a pearl. In his story, the actor is poor. Kino harvests pearls from the sea and sells them for a meager living. But one day he finds the pearl of all pearls, the pearl that will make him a wealthy man and educate his son. Suddenly, however, we see how earthly treasure corrupts. The generous poor man becomes a frightened stingy man, whose paranoia finally causes the death of his own son and several others. The treasure is an evil that has taken over his life, so Kino and his wife, Juana, holding the bundle containing their dead baby boy, walk to the sea and throw the pearl back into the water from whence it came.

It's interesting that, like Steinbeck, the Bible warns us about the corruption of wealth in stories of Solomon's excesses, the Rich Fool and the Unforgiving Servant. In this parable, however, the pearl of great value is not corrupting, but fulfilling and prized. Moreover, the pearl represents the kingdom, which is not wealth per se, but a thing of great value. Anything worth having is worth paying the cost. Perhaps it is significant that the pearl dealer is already a wealthy man, wealthy in money. Now he gives up his money to have wealth of a different sort.

Mystery and Discovery

Jesus used these three simple parables to reveal something about the hidden mysteries of life and life in the realm of heaven. In two of these parables, something is hidden; in the other, the actor is searching for something. When the woman mixes the yeast with three whole measures of flour, the yeast disappears into the flour, waiting to show itself in the rising of the dough. In fact, the Greek words used in Matthew that the NRSV translates as "mixed in with" really say "hid in."

There are also clear indications of the joy of discovery in these parables. In fact, Matthew even says it: ". . . like treasure hidden in a field, which someone found and hid; then in his joy . . ." (13:44). The parable of the Hidden Treasure doesn't, in that regard, recommend greed or duplicity, even though the man who finds the treasure hides it again until he can buy the field. Still, that question lingers in the parable and urges us to examine our own attitudes toward the things we value. Do we in fact value the realm of heaven, the coming reign of God, enough to "go for it"? And what should our attitude be about how we go for it?

The parable of the Pearl contains all these elements of hiddenness and mystery, discovery and joy; but it also highlights the element of wanting. If we want the realm of heaven badly enough, what are we willing to do to bring it about? There's an old rabbinic story about the Messiah. The story has it that, if only every Jew would keep the law for just one day, the Messiah would come. One can infer from the story that not everyone wants it that badly.

How badly do we want the kingdom to come? We pray for it every week at least: "Thy kingdom come." But do we pray those words automatically, without really and earnestly meaning it? And what do we imagine we're praying for? That is, what is this kingdom that we want to come? Note the implicit element of danger here. Maybe we don't know what we're asking for. The blessing is also a warning: may you get what you want.

It turns out that these three simple parables aren't so simple after all. To say "the kingdom of heaven is like . . ." isn't all that simple. In the first place, "like" is a comparison to something else, which is quite a different thing from the thing itself. Jesus didn't say "the kingdom of heaven is . . . ." He said it's "like . . ." In other words, we can't capture the kingdom in some nicely phrased description or declarative sentence.

Advent and Reversal . . .

Then, too, each of these three short parables hints at the advent of the kingdom. Do you remember the song from *West Side Story*? "Somethin's comin', somethin' good; I got a feeling a miracle's due, gonna come true, comin' to me!" And the song goes on to say that the coming miracle is just down the street, around the corner, under a tree. It's so close that it's almost tangible. Certainly, its coming is exciting. So it is with the coming reign of God. And these parables point that out in single simple sentences. There's also an element of reversal in each of them. Once again, what we see is what we get! What appears so simple and straightforward isn't. Our expectations are reversed. Add to this complication the sense of hiddenness and mystery in these brief parables, and, suddenly, there's a whole lot more going on than we'd suspect at first blush.

The parables call into question many, if not all, of the things we take for granted. They undermine the routine security of our accepted values and call us into the daring business of making new decisions in each and every moment of our living.

In the common, ordinary, and seemingly mundane parts of our daily routine, the parables break in. They call us to reexamine the ordinary, because they use ordinary images. And at the same time they call us to think about life anew, reversing our expectation of the ordinary. They call us to dislodge our comfort with all we take for granted, because they give us a glimpse of the coming realm of heaven. They're just not that simple.

I started with Ernest Hemingway. Let me end with William Faulkner. In his Nobel acceptance speech, Faulkner said that the answers to the riddle of life may be simple, but they're never easy. So too are the parables of Jesus. What seems simple . . . isn't. What seems easy . . . isn't. What seems ordinary is extraordinary. What seems safe is dangerous. What seems common is exciting. The coming of the realm of heaven is . . . Well, I s'pose it's like . . .

Ah, the simple things.

Discussion and Action

1. Have show and tell. Share your collections of small things that have the potential of becoming great things. How are these things like the kingdom of God?

2. Pray the Lord's Prayer together, a phrase at a time, with a moment of silence between each phrase. In that silent moment, rephrase the words you've just prayed together and speak them aloud. When you get to "Thy kingdom come," also think of an image or a definition for the kingdom. Speak it aloud.

3. How much of the kingdom depends on God's action? How much depends on human action (faithfulness and obedience).

4. Take turns describing your greatest joys in life. What sacrifices did you make to have them? If not a sacrifice, what would you call this price for joy?

5. What could yeast represent? God? The gospel? The kingdom? Faith? How does each act as leavening in real life?

6. In your opinion, what are the best things in life? In your group, make a common list of the things that you really value and would be willing to sacrifice for. What motivates you to work for such things? How much does God's judgment motivate you? How much does joy motivate you?

7. Which man in the twin parables of the treasure and the pearl made the bigger sacrifice? made the biggest gain? Which one had the greater joy? What do Matthew's parables tell us about who will make it into heaven?

8. Divide into three groups and quickly rewrite these parables in contemporary language. As a closing, read the revised parables to each other.

3

The Sower and the Seed
Matthew 13:1-23

Not all seed falls on good ground.

Personal Preparation

1. Read Matthew 13:1-9. What does it mean to you? After you've considered the parable, read the explanation of it in 13:18-23. How different is your understanding from the explanation given in Matthew 13:18-23? Does it matter that your understanding may be different from the explanation given in the text? Why or why not?

2. Read Matthew 13:10-17. When did scripture begin to make sense to you in your faith journey? How much were you able to understand as a child? as a youth? as an adult? What teachers or mentors helped you know something about the faith so that you could learn more? Have you known someone who was able to embrace the Christian faith with only the Bible to guide him or her?

3. Read the parable again, thinking of yourself as each kind of soil mentioned. What rocky times have you had in your faith? barren times? fruitful times? What kind of soil would you say you are now?

Understanding

The purpose of the Gospel of Mark is to reveal who the Messiah is. The purpose of Matthew, however, is to reveal the truth about salvation, beginning with the creation of the world, through the Exodus and the coming of Jesus, to the end of all time when God will reign and all God's promises will be fulfilled. The parables of Matthew 13 make up an entire discourse on the coming reign of God. In our previous session, the seed and leaven parables tell how God will gather in the people and make a church from something small and seemingly inconsequential. The parables of the jewels, as some writers call the pearl and treasure parables, tell how the righteous will face the end. The parable of the Sower, which begins the chapter and this session, is a parable of judgment in preparation for the end. Here is what will happen to false teachers, people of weak faith, and the righteous when the time comes. That time may be now.

The parable of the Sower is interesting for at least two reasons. It has an explanation, which most other parables don't have, and it's written in the form of an allegory. Later, we'll look at why the parable may have an explanation. First, let's look at what an allegory is and why the parable of the Sower is one. Three things define religious allegory.

1. Allegory is a form of story in which the people, things, and events have a one-for-one relationship to the people, things, and events they symbolize. In John Bunyan's famous *Pilgrim's Progress,* for instance, the main character is named Christian. I think I can say without giving anything away that he represents Christians! In the same way, the main character in medieval morality plays is often named "Everyman." We don't even need a hint here! For a more contemporary example, read C. S. Lewis's *The Chronicles of Narnia.* The quickest way to think about this aspect of allegory is to remember "this equals that."

2. Allegory is a form of story in which we need to know something in order to learn something. One almost has to be a Christian in order to understand what Bunyan is trying to teach about being a Christian in *Pilgrim's Progress.* We won't understand what equals what unless we are already familiar with the first what. Often the thing we know that we can build on is simple. In this case, everybody knows a little about planting seeds. One doesn't need a degree in agricultural engineering or horticulture to know

that seeds need good soil. But can we learn something about faith by knowing that pulling up weeds often uproots good plants, too?

3. Allegory is a form of story in which learning something is the whole point. In *Aesop's Fables*, the point is moral instruction; in *Pilgrim's Progress*, the point is Christian moral instruction. The author is intending to teach us something, usually a moral lesson, in an interesting and memorable way. Typically we can end an allegory by saying "and the moral of the story is . . . "

The parable of the Sower is not so clearly an allegory when it stands by itself (Matt. 13:1-9), but when Jesus explains the parable in verses 13-23, there is no mistaking the allegory. We are tempted to do the same with many other parables. Although it doesn't always work so well, we want to see obvious associations between characters in the parable and characters in real life. Take again the parable of the Unforgiving Servant. At the beginning, we quickly identify the king as God, and rightly so, because the king is just and gracious. However, by the end of the parable, we're not so likely to stick to this equation. The thought that God is a torturer is difficult to equate with the gracious God at the beginning of the parable. Parables are difficult to pin down. The most important thing to remember is "Let anyone with ears listen."

Morning Glories

The problem with allegories is that there is an exception to every rule. We can use an image like planting as long as seed behaves the same way every single time. But I remember the morning glories my mother planted between the walk and the garage. When they came up, Mom convinced Dad to build a trellis on the garage wall. The lovely green vines and leaves covered the trellis and the flowers burst forth every morning with a spray of colors ranging from white to lavender to red. That was the first year.

The next spring came, and Mom got so busy that she didn't replant the morning glories, but they came up anyway, filling the trellis again. And again, the green was lovely and the spray of colors was amazing. That was the second year.

The next spring, my folks put an addition on the house and moved the sidewalk. Mom rooted out the morning glories, but they came up nonetheless, only this time they didn't come up quite where she'd planted them. That year— and year after year— the volunteers came up here and there. They were persistent volunteers. Indefatigable volunteers. Unremovable volunteers. For years.

Maybe the parable means just what Jesus said it means in the explanation of the allegory. But maybe we would come to the same meaning ourselves, without explanation.

If It Works, Why Explain It?

There's an old rule among comedians that you should never explain a joke. If the audience doesn't get it, move on quickly. I've been watching the television reruns of the great episodes of the *Tonight Show* with Johnny Carson, and I've noticed that Carson often explained a joke. He'd tell it, and it would bomb. Nobody would laugh. But, instead of moving on, he'd stop and fumble around trying to explain it. Occasionally he'd even tell it again after the explanation. Carson is such a master that the explanation was almost always funnier than the joke. Failure raised to an art form!

I have to admit, though, that I'm a little disappointed this parable gets explained in the Gospels. The point of a parable is that a parable is the point. So why explain it? If it doesn't work, move on quickly. After all, there's nothing deadlier than explaining a joke, or, for that matter, a parable.

But explain it, they do—Matthew, Mark, and Luke. To be honest, I wonder whether it was really Jesus who explained it. He used parables so masterfully that no explanation was needed, and, more often, no explanation was appropriate. That is, the parables were intended to make us think. They were, as we've noted before, deceptively simple. A good part of the teaching that lies behind and within the parables is that the parables are *intended* to leave us hanging a bit and unsettled. The common, ordinary, daily-life details of the parable hook us, and then we're forced to make and remake decisions about our life that we too often take for granted.

The Purpose of the Parables

Sandwiched between the parable of the Sower and the explanation of it is a section that talks about the purpose of parables in general. Mark and Luke also contain this material. Each Gospel writer's explanation of the purpose of parables, however, is different. Since each has a different sense of the realm of God, each has a different purpose for the parable about the realm of God.

For one thing, Matthew has less of the urgency about the coming kingdom than does Mark. After all, Mark wrote his Gospel first (about 70 A.D.), when certainty about Jesus' return was running high. By the time Matthew wrote his Gospel about ten years later, Jesus had still not returned. Matthew believed it was time to place the emphasis on the organization of the new Christian community, since they were going to be around indefinitely. Of course, organizing the first church took time and required the development of rules and rituals. Matthew wanted to soften the urgency of Mark's Gospel as a way to give the community time to settle in to life in the world and to think of the realm of God as both something in the future and something happening now.

In Matthew, Jesus tells the parables to the crowd, but only the disciples truly understand what they mean. Jesus tells the parables almost as if they are a secret code for the disciples, which others can hear but not perceive. The disciples alone seem to be able to understand what Jesus is saying. In Mark, the opposite happens. The disciples hear, but they understand very little of what is ultimately going to happen. The disciples seem a little daft, so Mark has Jesus preaching the parables openly, hoping that anyone out there other than the disciples will understand. But in Matthew, Jesus faces growing opposition to his teachings and turns his attention to a small corp of twelve followers who understand him. They will become the seed on good ground that will grow up to be the church.

Matthew's explanation of the purpose of the parables includes a quotation from the prophet Isaiah that none of the other Gospel writers includes: "All this took place in order to fulfill what had been spoken by the Lord through the prophet (Matt. 1:22). One of the distinctive emphases of Matthew's Gospel is the

dependence upon the theme of fulfillment. Matthew is familiar
with the Septuagint, the Greek version of the Hebrew Bible, and
he searches out the texts that demonstrate its fulfillment in the
life and ministry of Jesus.

What About Matthew?

What about the explanation offered in Matthew 13:18-23? Where
does it come from?

Many scholars believe that the early church was just as un-
comfortable with the parables as were the people to whom Jesus
originally addressed them. In a time when the church was beginning to become the church and was learning how to live here and
now in an earthly society, it was too unsettling to leave the parables
alone. The church now had the task of defining and codifying its
teachings, both in order to "catechize" or teach its members
and to formulate a tradition that could be passed along to the
future generations.

So the explanation was taken up into the growing tradition.
Each Gospel writer put his own stamp on the story. Notice, for
instance, that only Mark (4:13) has Jesus chiding his listeners:
"Do you not understand this parable? Then how will you understand all the parables?" By the time we get to Matthew, there is
no more chastisement, and Matthew has Jesus moving directly
into the explanation (13:18-19).

The explanation allegorizes the parable, the very thing we are
tempted to do with many parables. The seed equals the word. The
birds equal "the evil one." Various kinds of ground equal the various kinds of listeners. And like other allegories, we have to know
something, in this case farming, in order to learn something. Finally, there's an obvious moral lesson at issue about receiving the
word and holding it fast, another sign of allegory.

Sometimes there are truths we just know. We can't explain
them, we can't paraphrase them, we can't analyze them. We just
experience them. There's a certainty about them that we can't
argue with, no matter how hard we try. It's like a story that means
a lot to us: sometimes we can't translate it for someone else. "You
just had to be there." It's like a novel that transports us out of the

world in which we live and places us squarely in the world it creates. And, that's the way it is when we live in parables.

Discussion and Action

1. Name movies or novels that leave you hanging with questions and confusion. Where would you go for an explanation?

2. What meaning did this parable have for you before it was explained? after? Why do you think Jesus explained this parable?

3. Who should understand the Christian faith? What is the bare minimum someone should understand about faith to call him or herself a Christian? Why do you think the disciples were able to understand when others could not?

4. Working alone or in small groups, write allegories to illustrate a moral point of your choosing. Use the three characteristics of allegory presented in the session to guide you. Read the allegories to each other.

5. In pairs or groups of three, talk about where you see yourselves in the parable. What kind of soil are you now? When in your life have you been barren, rocky, or fertile soil?

6. This is a parable of the kingdom, but it is also a parable of judgment. It says that when the reign of God begins, God will decide whether people are worthy to enter the kingdom. How does this picture of God square with your understanding of God?

7. If we are types of ground in this parable, what are the seeds? Who is the sower? Why doesn't the sower place all the seed on good ground?

8. What picture are you getting of the reign of God from the parable of the Sower, the parables of the Yeast and the Seed, and the parables of the Treasure and the Pearl? How does this picture fulfill the promises that God has made to save God's people?

4

Weeds, Wheat, and Fishnet
Matthew 13:24-30, 36-43, 47-50

Only God can decide whether we are righteous enough to enter into the kingdom.

Personal Preparation

1. Read Matthew 13:24-30, 36-43, 47-50. What do you believe about judgment? Will God judge the world? Will it come at the end? Is it happening now? How do you think you would fare? How does God the Judge fit together with God the Savior in your understanding?
2. Who are your enemies? Who or what distracts you from your faith? How well or how poorly are you able to resist the distractions?
3. Jesus cautions us against pulling up the weeds (our enemies) for fear that we will also uproot the wheat (the righteous). What, if anything, can you do about evil in the world if you cannot uproot it?
4. Be self-conscious this week about how often you or your family is judgmental of others. How can you curb yourselves of the habit of judging, which is God's responsibility?

Understanding

When I was growing up, I lived in the middle of the block in the upper half of a duplex on Marshall Avenue in St. Paul. At one corner stood First Christian Church; at the other stood St. Joseph's Academy for Girls. The neighborhood was located almost in the shadow of the St. Paul Cathedral and was populated mostly by second-generation Italian Catholics. The neighborhood was narrow from north to south and long from east to west. To the north was a black neighborhood. To the south was Summit Avenue where all the rich folks lived and beyond which was a predominantly Jewish neighborhood. Sometimes it seemed I was the only white Protestant around.

I wish that back then I'd known about Tom Lehrer's spoof on ethnic relations in his song "National Brotherhood Week" about white folks hating black folks and black folks hating whites; the Catholics hating the Protestants, the Protestants hating the Catho lics and everybody hating the Jews! Despite the civil rights movement, there was a lot of animosity, generally hidden, between and among the groups in the 1950s, as there is now.

As I look back, however, it's not the conflict I remember, but the rich diversity. It was a great gift to be able to listen to the Latin Mass, African American spirituals, and Hebrew chants a few yards from my house. When I came out of my front door on Sunday mornings, the persistent question for me was whether I should turn left and head to the east corner to go to Sunday school at First Christian or turn right toward the other corner and throw crab apples at the nuns with other unruly children. I say that, only partly facetiously, because wherever there is that kind of diversity—religious, social, or otherwise—there are serious questions about insiders and outsiders. Who's in, in terms of the kingdom of God, and how do we know? Who's out, and how do we know? And, most of all, who makes the decisions about who's in and who's out?

Judgment

Jesus teaches about judgment in the parable of Weeds Among the Wheat and the parable of the Fishnet. These parables are yet more stories in Matthew 13 about the kingdom, providing yet another glimpse of what God's reign is like. We have seen that the kingdom is a shelter with room enough (the mustard plant) and food enough (the leaven). We have seen how joy in the kingdom prompts us to give up all earthly treasure for the treasure of the kingdom (hidden treasure and pearls). And we have seen that only those who are receptive (good soil) to the gospel can truly benefit in God's reign. Now we will see through the parables of Wheat and Weeds and Fishnet that only God can decide whether we are righteous enough to enter into this realm.

Canned Tuna

I heard a commentary on National Public Radio the other day. The commentator was talking about tuna that is labeled "dolphin safe." You remember the controversy about netting tuna. Dolphins follow the tuna and the boats that fish for them. They often get caught up in the nets that are strung to catch the tuna, and, since dolphins are mammals, they die when they get caught in the nets and can't get back to the surface to breathe. Regulations were put into effect to protect the dolphins, which seemed to be working relatively well. Apparently, however, the regulations minimized but did not eliminate the problem. Dolphins were still getting killed. This commentator wanted "absolutely dolphin safe" tuna.

Whether or not that's possible in the world of fishing, the parables for this session tell us it's not possible in the world of fishing for people. When it comes to insiders and outsiders, those who'll get into the kingdom and those who won't, who decides which ones are keepers and which ones have to be thrown back? Can the ones we don't want in the "net" be sorted out before the catch is hauled in? Can the undesirable plants be weeded out before the harvest? Both of this week's parables ask those questions.

Insiders and Outsiders

In the parable of Weeds Among the Wheat, the disciples want to know if they should root out the weeds (detractors from the faith) from the wheat (the righteous). Wouldn't it be better, they reason, to expel the evil element from the church before they pollute the whole group? Jesus, also thinking of the emerging little church, emphatically says no. In the parable of the Fishnet, he reminds the disciples that the nets are only drawn in when they are full (an allusion to the theme of fulfillment?); and when they are drawn in, all kinds of fish, good and bad, are hauled in together. Only at the end of the fishing process are the different fish separated. In the parable of the Weeds Among the Wheat, he reminds the disciples that good plants often come uprooted with the bad plants in the process of weeding. It is better to wait until all the plants are mature and then separate them at the harvest.

In the explanations attached to both parables, Jesus explains that weeds and bad fish are the forces working against the faith. In the wheat and weeds, this unruly force is led by an enemy who slips in and sows the weeds when everyone else is asleep. A few verses later, we find that the enemy is the devil and the weeds are the children of the evil one. The Greek word *diabolos*, translated as devil, means "slanderer." It is used six times in Matthew's Gospel, four times in the fourth chapter, once in the twenty-fifth, and once here in the thirteenth. The "devil"—not the stereotypical character in the red suit with horns, tail, and pitchfork, but more likely someone just like us—is the one who corrupts the word with slander and lies.

The catch of fish, like the crop of wheat, is also polluted by evil. The word for "bad" has immediate application to fish; it translates as crumbling, decayed, or rotten—an apt description of bad fish! In fact, Ephesians 4:29 the word *bad* is used to mean corrupt. This corruption is not something that is out there in the world, from which we are safe in the church. Corruption has entered even the church, and the disciples want to know what they should do about it.

It's natural to want to do something about it. I live in Nebraska, land of expansive fields, center-pivot irrigation, corn and beans and milo as far as the eye can see and beyond. When the milo is beautiful shades of rust and brown and gold and red and ripe for harvest, it's easy to pick out the volunteer corn or sunflowers that have sprouted from seed from last year. And I know enough about farming to know that black nightshade stains a load of soy beans when you harvest them, making them less valuable at market, so farmers must "walk beans," which is the practice of walking down long rows of soy beans, pulling out volunteers and weeds before harvest. We all want to improve the harvest, to get rid of the thing that is polluting the crop.

It's a little surprising, then, when Jesus says no, we must not uproot the weeds before the harvest, and we must not separate the bad fish from the good before the whole catch is brought in. These two parables are about judgment—kingdom judgment—not human judgment. Kingdom judgments are best left to God or the angels at the end of time. But, as Shakespeare said, there's the rub.

Kingdom Judgments and Dead Armadillos

How often are we like the harvest workers, who want to pull the weeds and get rid of them? Very likely you have an irritant or troublemaker in your congregation whom you'd like to put out. There is at least one in mine—it could even be me. It may be somebody who is just plain difficult to get along with, or it could be someone whose beliefs seem dangerous and beyond the pale of Christian belief. Pollution takes all kinds of forms.

In one congregation where I served as pastor, we welcomed a wonderful woman as a member. She had a son that we didn't know about at first. He was in his twenties and had moved in and out of the home, but he was back home with his mother for the time being. What I soon discovered was that he'd been "away" in a mental health facility. He suffered from schizophrenia, a brain disorder with symptoms that manifest themselves in behavior problems.

On some Sundays, this young man would jump up during worship and begin to yell fire and brimstone judgments, usually, about the world and the people in it, including our congregation. Several people in the congregation were quite upset about his disruption, because they sincerely believed worship needed to be carried on with decorum and propriety. I didn't know what to do. I understood his disease, and I was acutely aware of the pain it caused his mother. And yet I sympathized with the feelings of members of my congregation. I was really caught.

Several in my congregation worked with people who had developmental disabilities. In fact, we were the church home for a special group of these men and women who lived in a local group home and called themselves "Jesus' Eagles." This congregation was as open, warm, and accepting as any congregation I have every known, except when it came to this occasional problem with decorum.

The story doesn't have a happy ending. The young man left, just disappeared, before the matter was resolved. We got rid of the "weed," but we also lost the "wheat" when his mother moved to another town. In hindsight I wish I had done things differently. Like the disciples I felt something ought to be done, but all along I was thinking that we needed to gracefully "pull up" the weed and cast it away. If I had been thinking like Jesus, I would have worked with the congregation to overcome our temptation to judge.

Can we really live without judging, though? In fact, we do make judgments about others every day. It's a necessity of getting through the week. A boss makes judgments about her employees; parents make judgments about their children; kids make judgments about their friends. We parents discipline our children for their transgressions, real or imagined. And according to Richard Nelson Bolles, the jobs expert, most of us will change jobs (even careers) nearly a dozen times during our working lives, most of which will come at someone else's request. Judgments are a fact of life, by us and about us.

The Matthean parables we've read are quite unsettling. There are no easy answers, no clear rules or guidelines. We've got to live with them awhile. We've got to hang on to them and not let them go so easily.

Weeds in the Wheat . . .

What are we to do in the meantime? How do we as Christians live with the weeds in the wheat? When something smells to high heaven (pun intended), like the rotten fish, what do we do? The advice of the householder to his servants isn't very satisfying, especially to those of us with a penchant for neat and orderly fields. It's so difficult not to pull weeds.

Perhaps we're less likely to pull weeds, and the wheat with it, if we face into the question whether we ourselves are weeds or wheat. One of the most faithful Christians I've ever been privileged to know describes himself as a bum, a sinner. Even though I've almost literally never witnessed him falling short of a profoundly faithful and ethical response to life, he insists he's a bum. For sure, by virtue of God's grace, he is a valuable and valued human being. He is loved. He is precious. He is good. But by his own admission, he has fallen short of the glory of God.

I keep wondering, If he's a bum, what am I? I feel he's far better than I and he's a sinner. That must make me a worse sinner, even though I too believe that God loves me. The God who can and does love me, despite my evident undeserving, must then also love and value the difficult ones, the impossible ones, the mixed-up ones, and the wrong headed ones. Which one of us then is to judge? Where could you and I possibly draw the line between who's in and who's out?

I received a gift that, over the years, I've made my own. It's a benediction I got from Rollie Martinson, a Lutheran family systems therapist and teacher. I'll pass it on to you.

> Until that time when God makes everything whole and full and complete, may the gracious spirit of God live in you and among you, that you may know and be known, love and be loved, care and be cared for—as you live life in between.

Because that is where life is. Life is somewhere between parables and canned tuna.

Discussion and Action

1. What ideas did you come up with in preparation for this session to help you restrain yourself from making judgments that are God's to make?

2. Can you think of judgments about others that seem necessary or unavoidable? Can you define any kinds or categories of judgments that good Christians need to make about others? Do any of them have to do with people "not like us"?

3. How does your congregation accept members into the church? What judgments are made about a person's readiness to join the church? Who makes those judgments? How is it possible or impossible to abuse that authority to judge?

4. In Matthew 18, Jesus tells us how to discipline each other in the church. How is discipline different from judgment? How could discipline have helped the congregation dealing with the mentally ill member? Where can the best of us and the worst of us use discipline in our lives?

5. As a group, write a corporate confession. Then talk about the assurance of pardon and forgiveness you would like to receive from God. If there is someone in the group who can do so, have that person pronounce the forgiveness and offer the group a blessing. If not, say the confession together and offer each other a blessing.

6. When in all of church history (including recent history) has the church been endangered by evil, wrong belief, and enemies? What did church leaders do? When in church history have Christians abused the power to judge others? Make a list of incidents you know of. What has the church learned about judging others over the course of history?

7. Examine your own prejudices. Prejudice is to prejudge, to judge based on stereotypes and generalities. Where and how in your communities are people the victims of prejudice? in the schools? in businesses? in houses of worship? in sports complexes and recreation areas? Pinpoint leaders in the community who could address the problem. Choose someone in the group to convey the covenant group's concern to a community leader.

5

The Seeking Shepherd and the Lost Sheep
Matthew 18:10-14

As God, out of incredible love for each one of us, searches to bring us back into the fold, so we too should love one another that much.

Personal Preparation

1. Read Matthew 18:1-20, concentrating on verses 10-14. What does the parable of the Lost Sheep say to you about God? If God were to find you and return you to the "fold," who else would be in that fold?

2. Matthew 18:6-7 talks about stumbling blocks. Think about a time you may have been a stumbling block for someone seeking faith? Who stood in your way on your personal journey of faith?

3. What are the rules, written and unwritten, for relationships in your family? What system do you have for communicating, showing respect to others, and confronting family members? What systems did you have in the family of your childhood?

4. What is the worst offense someone has committed against you personally? How have you possibly offended others? How were these situations resolved?

Understanding

Between the parables of chapter 13 and the next set of parable teachings in chapter 18, Matthew tells many stories of Jesus. John the Baptizer has been executed. Jesus feeds five thousand people and walks on water. Peter confesses his faith. Jesus defends himself and his disciples against the attacks of scribes and Pharisees. He commends the faith of a Canaanite woman, feeds four thousand people, and offers the keys of the kingdom to Peter. He predicts his passion, is transfigured on the mountain, heals the sick, and exorcizes a demon from a young boy. Now that's quite a list!

If you look quickly through this section, you will see in chapters 14–15 that Jesus is teaching and preaching to crowds of people, would-be followers. Then in chapters 16–17 Jesus begins to "combat" the religious authorities and turn almost exclusively to his disciples to teach and preach. This shift is a crucial turning point. Knowing that his own death is imminent, Jesus prepares the new community, the church, to go on after him. The stories of chapters 16–17, stories of people of great faith and people with little or no faith, establish who is truly in relationship with God (and therefore in the community) and who is not.

This new community that is coming together needs guidelines for relating, which is what we get in chapter 18. Chapter 18 is all about how to live in community, beginning with how not to offend each other. Be humble, not brash, stop putting stumbling blocks before other people, and stop offensive behavior that puts others off.

Chapter 18 begins a new discourse, though its introduction really begins at the end of chapter 17 with the story of the temple tax (Matt. 17:24-27). Jesus and Simon Peter have a brief conversation about paying the temple tax. If Matthew was written around 80 A.D., the Jerusalem temple was already destroyed, but the Roman emperor still collected a tax from Jewish males for war reparations and support of Roman temples. The tax collectors want to know from Peter whether his leader, Jesus, pays the temple tax. Jesus uses a double entendre to say that God's people do not owe anyone anything. Not even the Romans would collect a tax from children, and they, being children of God, therefore do not have any obligation to the Romans. However, Jesus counsels Peter to not offend unnecessarily and to pay the tax, knowing it does not ultimately obligate them to anything. Perhaps keeping the Romans happy allows Jesus' community some freedom from scrutiny.

Twin Gospels

Matthew is written later than the Gospel of Mark and uses a lot of Mark's material, but the two Gospel accounts are different. While Mark shows Jesus working with Gentiles and outsiders, Matthew works mainly through the disciples who seemingly understand better who Jesus is and what's happening than the disciples described in Mark. In this regard Matthew's view of the disciples is decidedly more optimistic than Mark's.

Whereas Mark's Gospel is almost sparse in its narrative, Matthew, on the other hand, adds the genealogy and the birth narrative at the beginning and the resurrection appearance and Great Commission at the end. In addition, he lengthens many of the stories taken from Mark, e.g., the healing of one person becomes the healing of many persons.

Matthew also emphasizes the organization of the believing community, the church. Remember that Matthew is the only Gospel writer who uses the word *ekklesia*, or church. The best examples here are Jesus' pronouncement that Peter will be the rock on which Jesus will build the church (Matt. 16:13-20) and the rules for life in the new community (Matt. 18). It's almost as if Matthew wanted to write the constitution and bylaws!

In one parish I served, we needed to rewrite the articles of incorporation and the bylaws. It's easier for me if I think of them less as laws and more as guidelines for relationship. When I proposed that we revise the sentence on membership, I suggested we use, "Membership in this congregation includes all those who, in every time and place, proclaim the lordship of Jesus Christ." Even though we went on to limit voting privileges to those "on the rolls," it was my intention to connect our people with the universal church, the great cloud of witnesses that surrounds us: Peter and Augustine and Theresa of Avila and Martin Luther, as well as

Alexander Campbell of the Disciples and Alexander Mack of the Brethren. After a lot of debate, it passed.

We filed the revised articles of incorporation with the Secretary of State's office. We got an almost immediate reply, You can't do that! We asked, Why not? After a long delay, they answered, We don't know. Finally, they accepted the revised articles that claim our relationship with all those who in every time and place proclaim Jesus as Lord! It was a little victory for the view that church bylaws are laws as much as they are an attempt to follow Jesus in the way we relate to each other. That's not something the state knows how to do, or apparently, how to handle.

Parables of Relationship

This week, we begin talking about the parables of relationship in Matthew 18, though it seems like the chapter quickly turns to focus on broken relationships. But that's not all bad. We all have disagreements with other people. We all have conflict at one time or another in life. In many ways, conflict is at the very heart of our relationships, all our relationships, even our relationship with God. Though relationships may be turbulent at times, they are undoubtedly better than no relationships at all.

Elie Wiesel tells the story of the man who cleans the synagogue and lights the candles. He's an ordinary guy, but he has great insights into human behavior. People come to him for advice; they tell him their life story, they tell him all about their conflicts and relationships and their struggles of faith. At one point, he tells someone that we respond three ways in our relationship with God. There's the "yes" in obedience, and that's okay. There's the "no in thunder," and that's okay too. The only one that isn't okay is indifference.

Rules for Relationships

The rules for relationships in Matthew 18 are a response to conflict that Jesus sees among the disciples and in the church. He's not talking about conflict with "enemies" such as the Pharisees or occupying forces such as the Romans. He's talking about the children of God. They're human too. You can imagine the disciples bickering over who is greatest or throwing a stumbling block in the path of another Christian in their eagerness to stay close to Jesus. The church, just like any other group, has to learn to communicate.

Jesus says, "Occasions for stumbling are bound to come" (18:7). I can attest to that. One evening my wife and I got into an argument. We were sitting in front of the television, eating dinner on TV trays, and it started. Later, we couldn't even recall what it was about, but it was nasty. We snapped back and forth at each other; dinner was a disaster; and we missed the news.

When we calmed down and talked about things, we made a startling discovery: we had been arguing about the doggone TV trays! You see, in Jan's family everything stopped for dinner at precisely five o'clock. She and her mom and dad and brother spent the hour around the dinner table doing family business, that is, building relationships. In my family, we often had a long drive to church and back each week, which gave us the same amount of time to do our family business, that is, building relationships. In the relatively new household Jan and I were establishing, neither of our family traditions was being served. The TV trays got in the way.

All of a sudden, the "stumbling block" verses made real sense to me. The worthless TV trays were clearly the stumbling block, because they kept us from paying attention to family business, doing what we needed to do. When we moved to a new house in another state, the one thing we insisted on was that the house had to have a dining room. Nothing is more important than working on family relationships. The same can be said of maintaining relationships in the family of God.

The Lost Sheep
The parables of Matthew 18 give us help in how to relate to each other by following the example of God in Jesus Christ. Doesn't God forgive endlessly, like the king in the parable of the Unforgiving Servant? And doesn't God search endlessly for the ones among us who have gone astray? We then should also forgive brothers and sisters endlessly and search for strayed people tire-

lessly. The parable of the Lost Sheep might be read as a story of salvation and our duty to bring in unsaved souls, but its main purpose is to reveal something of who God is. God is the shepherd who, out of incredible love for each one of us, will leave ninety-nine sheep in the mountains unattended to find one lost sheep and bring it back to the fold. God loves us that much, and we ought to love one another in the community that much as well.

A Hierarchy of Healing

Between the parables in Matthew 18 is a practical, systematic approach to dealing with conflict in the church. It tells us how to lovingly bring someone back into the fold in a four-step, graduated process.

The system is specifically for confronting broken relationships. We're talking about sins "against" someone else, not merely sinning in the sense of breaking religious laws. Jesus is not asking the church to tattle on others, pointing a blaming finger and demanding that So-and-So account for it! The system applies to those occasions when someone has offended someone else. And the first step is for the aggrieved to go privately to the one who has offended and try to mend the broken relationship. At this point discretion is important.

What do we do when confronting the offender is not enough? The next step in the process is to visit the offender again, this time with a witness. Unfortunately, we think of witnesses in the context of a trial, but that's not what the text means here. The witnesses are really helpers, present to support and assist both parties in mending the relationship. Today, we would call them mediators, though Matthew's mediator is not an objective, disinterested third party; he or she is fully invested in bringing a member of the community back to the fold.

We and our children sometimes play that role for each other. When my fourteen-year-old daughter's world falls apart, I have a little litany. I ask: "Are you going to die? Is somebody else going to die?" Usually that outsider's view helps to put the "end of the world" in perspective for her.

Once, I came home from an especially bad day at the office. Nothing had gone right and, it seemed to me, everything had gone wrong. I fussed and fumed around the house, griping and grumbling at this and that and being a general pain in the posterior. At the height of my tirade, my daughter walked up and said: "Are you going to die? Is somebody else going to die?" What a witness!

Tell It to the Church

Suppose the aggrieved person and the witnesses are unable to resolve the issue. The next stage is to go to the church. This step has often been misconstrued as a requirement to confess sins publicly and undergo public judgment. There was a famous case in Texas where a woman's "sins," confessed to her pastor, were announced to the congregation. My recollection is that the elders of that congregation asked the people to join in pronouncing judgment on the woman. She sued.

That's not what the text means. The church is, in Matthew's report of Jesus' vision of it, the caring community of people gathered in Christ's name. They are family, in the best sense of the word. Telling it to the church, in this context, has the same burden as offering a prayer request. Telling it to the church enlists the congregation in the solution to the problem, not in the judgment of the "sinner." Telling it to the church provides a community of wisdom and support at a time when people are most vulnerable, in the midst of a broken relationship.

Anathema

But sometimes even the whole congregation cannot bring about a resolution, which brings us to the last step, the one we'd rather not hear: "Let such a one be to you as a Gentile and a tax collector" (18:17). This doesn't sound like much of a threat to us, but in Jesus' time and place, Jews didn't associate with Gentiles, and first-century tax collectors were worse than IRS agents. Yet Jesus associated with both of these groups. So are we to turn them out in the final step, or bring them in and love them anyway? If we're going to treat one another as Gentiles and tax collectors, maybe we should love them and touch them and heal them and eat with them.

Notice how the section ends. "Truly I tell you, whatever you bind on earth will be bound in heaven, and whatever you loose on earth will be loosed in heaven" (18:18). With this ending Jesus places the authority and the responsibility for administering the rules of relationship in the hands of his followers. That's you and me, fallible and frail and cantankerous and sinful as we are. We're his sheep, and sheep aren't always very bright, but at least they know enough to stick together. You see, it's the relationship that matters, the community of faith that counts, the mutual love and support that endures.

"For, wherever two or three are gathered together in my name, I am there among them." Loving us. Touching us. Healing us. Eating with us—Gentiles and tax collectors.

Discussion and Action

1. What does Jesus mean when he says "unless you change and become like children you will never enter the kingdom of heaven"? In what way should we in the church be like children?

2. Talk about stumbling blocks to faith you have encountered in your own life. Then think about your congregation. What stumbling blocks does it present to people seeking faith? What language stumbling blocks do you have? building accessibility? theological positions? worship style?

3. What offending things in your church building or church community should be "cut off" or cast away? How difficult is it to do that? Why is it difficult to do that in your personal life?

4. Who are the least and the lost in your congregation? How does your congregation care for these people? Tell stories from your personal experience of people who were lost from the congregation and were brought home. What was the homecoming like?

5. The parable of the Lost Sheep doesn't tell us if the shepherd put any conditions on the sheep's return to the fold.

What conditions, if any, should a congregation put on the
return of a lost member? If we should not name the conditions under which a person can return, why not?

6. Look at your congregational constitution or bylaws. What
provision is there in the document for confronting offending members or settling disputes? How well or poorly
has the church handled these confrontations?

7. What kinds of relational problems can be confronted by
the four-step process in Matthew 18:15-20? Share examples from personal experience. What kinds of "sins"
would better be confronted another way? How should
they be confronted? Who should do it? Invite the pastor
to talk with the group on church discipline—whose responsibility is it? What constitutes a sin? What is the end
goal of church discipline?

8. Read again the parable of the Lost Sheep. What would
you say is the end goal of the four-step process in Matthew 18 in light of the parable? What is the ultimate goal
of church discipline in your congregation?

6

The Unforgiving Servant
Matthew 18:21-35

*Forgive and forgive and forgive some more. Forgive
well beyond your ability to count the times.*

Personal Preparation

1. Read Matthew 18:21-35. Think about which is easier for
   you, being forgiven or forgiving another. What makes it
   difficult to forgive? to be forgiven?
2. Take out all your credit cards and line them up on the
   table in front of you. On a piece of paper, estimate the
   amounts you owe on each of them and total the amounts.
   How does that debt make you feel? Does anyone owe
   you anything? Why would you or would you not consider forgiving that debt?
3. Whose forgiveness do you need? How can you go about
   asking for it?
4. Who needs your forgiveness? How willing are you to
   give it?

Understanding

Bob Cratchet can never seem to do anything quite right, if you
listen to Scrooge. In Dickens' time, most everybody in the upper
crust knew and read the Bible, but we have to wonder if Scrooge
ever read the parable of the Unforgiving Servant in Matthew. Finally, after Scrooge's own encounter with grace, we finally see

him come around in the story, maybe even seven times seventy times. But then again, can't you just see Scrooge saying, "That's four hundred and eighty-nine."

Forgiving and Forgetting

Do you forgive easily, or is it difficult for you? I suppose it depends on the circumstances, how seriously you have been wronged. I once knew an old Scrooge who insisted that he would gladly forgive anybody anything. But he wouldn't forget.

Does forgiving involve forgetting? What is forgiveness? These are questions that underlie the parable of the Unforgiving Servant, which Jesus told in response to Peter's question "Lord, how often should I forgive?" Only the Gospel of Matthew contains this parable, which is consistent with Matthew's emphasis on relationships and rules within the believing community. Like the rest of Matthew 18, it deals with problems of relationship where someone has offended someone else. While forgiveness may also be in order for all sins, this parable deals with offenses against others in the church.

In the story that prompts the parable, Peter asks Jesus how many times he should forgive an offending brother or sister—as many as seven times? Seven times seems ample, and besides, seven is a number in the Bible that symbolizes fullness and completeness. Peter likely thought he was going beyond what was expected by saying seven.

While seven seems good, anyone who has tried to raise kids knows it's not enough! Kids seem to persist in their mistakes, making them over and over again. In fact, sometimes it seems that they not only persist, but insist on their errors. Parents get so frustrated with their kids they could tear their hair out. In our sane moments, we parents realize that kids are just testing the limits, pushing the boundaries, and that they will learn a great deal from this. That's how they mature. That's how they develop the capacity for sound judgment.

But saying that is a whole lot easier in retrospect than it was at the time. Am I right? How often are we tempted to say, "Seventy-seven times and counting!" Notice that Bible translators translate the number differently. I grew up reading "seventy times seven," or 490 times. The NRSV says seventy-seven times in the text and seventy times seven in a footnote. Translations differ because the ancient texts differ, but the point is the same. Forgive and forgive and forgive some more. Forgive well beyond your ability to count the times.

Easier Said Than Done

After Jesus gives Peter a straightforward answer, he tells a parable. A servant begs and receives his master's forgiveness for a huge debt, then turns around and refuses to forgive the minor amounts owed by his own debtors. Upon hearing this, his master reverses his original decision, reinstates the servant's debt, and even has the servant tortured until he pays up.

For a number of reasons, this is a very disturbing parable, not the least of which is the anger and torture that are part of it. How in the world can this situation be like the kingdom of heaven? In the Hebrew Bible, it was not uncommon for a debtor to be sold into slavery to pay off the debt. In Jesus' time, it wasn't uncommon for debtors to be jailed for their refusal or inability to pay their debts. Indeed, debtors' prisons were still around in England and other places until this century. In the United States and Canada today, debts can lead to bad credit ratings, garnishment of wages, and, in some cases, incarceration. But we would not likely claim that any of these places is like the kingdom of heaven.

The Hebrew Bible indicates how great a problem debt was. It mentions debts and debtors only nine times, but almost every mention is important. (The New Testament mentions debts and debtors eleven times, six of which are here in Matthew.) The Hebrew Bible has rules for indebtedness, with regulations about repayment. It also has rules about the forgiveness of debt, the most famous being the fiftieth year Jubilee when debts are to be waived.

The most common notion of debt in the Bible, however, is a theological concept. Even the social provision for Jubilee is done in imitation of the way God forgives us. We can't forget that God redeemed an undeserving people out of slavery, a debt we can never repay. More importantly, Jesus is a "ransom" paid for us, another debt we can never repay. As the hymn says, "Oh to grace how great a debtor daily I'm constrained to be."

It's interesting to note that the remission of debt is tied to the notion of relationship, the issue we dealt with in the last session. We are, after all, still in the chapter on church relations, and Jesus is continuing a lesson on getting along. The strategic placement of teachings on forgiveness after teachings on church discipline suggests that the two are connected. We must admonish each other and discipline members who offend, but then we must also forgive. The goal of discipline, after all, is to bring people back, to restore the community. That can't happen unless forgiveness is part and parcel with confrontation.

In this sense, the master's willingness to set aside the servant's debt is both an act of generosity and an act of religious obligation. In turn, the servant's unwillingness to remit the debts owed him shows both his "hard-hearted" and "tight-fisted" (Deut. 15:7) attitude and his faithlessness. No wonder it fuels his master's anger!

My Debt's Bigger Than Your Debt

Remember that Jesus was talking to common folk, the very people more likely to have debts to their masters. They would have identified more readily with the servants than the master. The question, of course, is to what extent they would have seen themselves as the unforgiving servant. Some have argued that it might even have been difficult for people to identify with any of the characters in the parable, since the amounts owed are so large (many lifetimes of wages). My guess is that, no matter with whom and to what extent the hearers identified, they certainly would have understood the story. We understand it at our core, whether we see ourselves as the indebted slave or the unforgiving former slave.

Farmers are one group who may be able to see all sides of the debt dilemma. In the 1970s and early 1980s, farmers were encouraged to expand their operations by borrowing. Many fell victim to the allure. Some farmers even feel the government encouraged them to take on too much debt. In any case, the rural crisis of the 1980s, which continues well into the '90s, was a whirlpool of debt, high interest rates, and low commodity prices that sucked many family farms under. The media covered horrible scenes of farm foreclosures and auctions, with bankers and creditors standing by, demanding repayment and forcing people off their land. Farm families stood by with silent tears, watching generations of work evaporate.

There's a lithograph that haunts me. It shows a group of farmers milling around the farm yard, looking at the machinery that is up for auction. Nearby, you can see the owner, hands stuffed in the pockets of his jeans, seed cap pulled down on his forehead, boots picking at the dust beneath his feet, shoulders slumped, waiting to witness his life and livelihood sold to the highest bidder.

The human dimension of debt is unsettling, its human face is unnerving. Creditors don't grab debtors by the throat and bodily threaten them. They are genuine, sympathetic people, doing their jobs. But, in some rural and small town congregations, creditors and farmers don't share the same pews any more. One farm wife told me that she didn't even go to church any longer because of the way folks stared at her.

The embarrassment, the anger, the shame, the sympathy—these are all very real emotions for debtors and creditors alike. It's not a great stretch for us to imagine all this behind the brief parable that Jesus offers in response to Peter's question. We applaud the master's generous and forgiving spirit. We get furious with the unforgiving servant. We identify with the poor victims of the servant's insensitivity. And we might even be tempted to approve of the master's response when he learns about what has happened. But how is this scenario like the kingdom of heaven?

Forgiveness, Sin, and Judgment

The subject here is forgiveness. If the king in the parable so readily forgives the indebtedness of his servant, we should readily understand our obligation to forgive as well: "Forgive us our debts, as we forgive our debtors." To say that another way, "God, as you have forgiven us, may we forgive those who are indebted to us." In this respect, of course, the parable is like the kingdom of heaven.

The parable is also like the kingdom of heaven in that sin is pardonable. God's realm is not without sin; it is *with* pardon. The very servant who has just been forgiven turns around and refuses to forgive others. Jesus acknowledges in the teaching on stumbling blocks (18:6-7) that there will be these occasions for sins against one another, but in the kingdom great weight is given to overcoming sin with grace and forgiveness.

The troubling part of the parable continues to be the final judgment against the unforgiving servant. In fact, there is more than judgment, which we can probably all understand; there's punishment, imprisonment, and even torture. That's one of the reasons that John Dominic Crossan suggests that the parable isn't really a good response to Peter's question. Will God in the kingdom of heaven really torture us for our sins? The founder of the Brethren, Alexander Mack, believed that God would restore all sinners in the last judgment, but he didn't talk about his belief much, fearing that others would think this glorious grace was license to behave badly, knowing that all would be saved in the end. Perhaps Matthew gives us the same caution. Do not think that because forgiveness is available, we are free to sin.

In this parable it is tempting to equate the king to God, who is endlessly forgiving and gracious. The problem comes, however, in reconciling the king who forgives the huge debt with the king at the end of the parable who sends the unforgiving servant to the torture chamber for a comparatively small debt. Can God be both tirelessly forgiving and, at the same time, fearsome and judgmental? I suppose anything is possible with God, but what are we to learn about true forgiveness in this parable? It's a difficult parable to work out.

My own best guess is that, as parable scholar Dan Otto Via remarks, the whole parable is the point. That is, we can't pick out one element or theme and say: Ah, there's the point. It's too easy to say that the point is that God will withdraw forgiveness from us if we withhold forgiveness from others. If it's just that, we can dust off our hands and move on.

Parables don't let us off that easily. They keep asking questions, or in this case, holding up a mirror before us. "The point" is that we see ourselves in all the elements of the parable. We see ourselves, certainly, in the sin of the unforgiving servant and are led to ask ourselves whether we really forgive, let alone forget. We also see ourselves in the other servants, because we've all been burdened by the oppression of indebtedness, literally or figuratively, and we've all been threatened, internally if not externally, by the weight of that burden. But we also see ourselves in the king, both in his better moments of generosity and, unfortunately, in his meaner moments of anger and retribution. It is we, not God, who can be generous one minute and vengeful another.

The Unforgivable Sin

There's a biblical reference to an unforgivable sin. But is there really such a thing? What, for example, do we do about an utterly recalcitrant, unrepentant sinner? Are there some sins you and I are more willing to forgive than others? What about child abuse? What about the Holocaust? Can we forgive Eichmann? Is there sin that only God can forgive?

Forgiveness isn't a simple matter after all. It goes against some of our deepest, and sometimes basest, instincts that make us human. And, as the parable teaches us, forgiveness is difficult because it clearly requires a prior step—repentance. We can't see ourselves as forgivers unless we see ourselves as forgiven. But we can't see ourselves as forgiven unless we see ourselves as sinners—repentant sinners.

Discussion and Action

1. When have you asked the question that Peter asked Jesus, "Lord, how often should I forgive?" If you are able, tell about occasions from your life in which you were called to forgive.
2. Under what conditions, if any, are you most willing to forgive? How does forgiving without any conditions make you feel?
3. It's difficult to forgive sometimes. How difficult is it to be forgiven? Jesus provides a process for practicing discipline. Brainstorm together a process for asking forgive-

ness and a process for granting forgiveness, starting with
repentance (the recognition that God has forgiven you).

4. What danger is there in knowing that God is endlessly
   forgiving? If God is so forgiving, why do you think more
   people in the world don't behave badly?

5. Look at each character in the parable: the king, the servant, and the servant's debtor. In what ways are we like
   all three?

6. Pray the Lord's Prayer together. When you get to the
   "debts and debtors" part, pause to name both the debts
   you have been forgiven and the debtors you need to forgive. If you say "trespasses," talk about the difference
   between debts and trespasses.

7. Sing "Come, thou fount" (p. 103) or "Amazing grace"
   (p. 104) as a way of recognizing that God forgives us and
   expects us to forgive others.

8. Talk about capital punishment and whether or not there
   are unforgivable sins. Or plan to gather at someone's home
   in the near future to watch the movie *Dead Man Walking.*
   Discuss it in the context of forgiveness.

7

Hard Messages: The Laborers in the Vineyard
Matthew 20:1-15; 21:28-32

Thankfully, God's grace overrides the database of judgments we maintain for ourselves and others.

Personal Preparation

1. Read Matthew 20:1-15 and 21:28-32. To see these parables in context, read 19:1–21:32. Think about your own mortality. How would you judge yourself if today was the last day of your life? How do you think God would judge you?
2. Which characters are you most like in these parables? In what ways?
3. By what criteria do you judge yourself? others? By what criteria does God judge?
4. How generous are you? What makes it difficult to be generous? Why, if at all, is it difficult to believe that God is generous?

Understanding

God is not fair. God is better than fair. God is generous. The parables for this session are parables of judgment in which Jesus tells how rewards will be handed out to the righteous and unrighteous alike. We have moved from parables describing the kingdom, which Jesus told in his traveling ministry, to parables of relationship, which Jesus used to illustrate how the church is to operate. Now, Jesus' ministry is drawing to a close, provisions have been made for the establishment of the church, and Jesus is heading toward Jerusalem and ultimately toward a judgment against him and to his own death and resurrection. In this context Jesus begins to teach the parables of judgment.

For the third time, Jesus foretells his passion (Matt. 20:17-19). Tensions are high between Jesus and Jewish and Roman authorities, and people are beginning to sense that the end is truly near. Not only do they sense that the end is near for Jesus, they talk of the end of the world. What does the teacher say about the fast approaching last judgment? What will happen to them? Who will be first in heaven? Who will sit at Jesus' right hand? One of our parables is a response to this question as the disciples ask it, and the other is a response to the question as the chief priests and elders ask it. Not surprisingly, Jesus' response is different in each case.

Still Waiting

The final judgment has still not come, so we, like the disciples, are also asking what will happen to us in the end. No matter how much we ask, though, the answer is still the same and it's still unexpected: God is generous with grace.

That's the answer I got as a boy of about thirteen or fourteen when I helped the gas company lay pipe in our neighborhood. No more propane tanks (we called them "pigs") in the back yard! The workers hired me to cut the threads on the pieces of pipe they needed for all the connections. I got a nickel a thread, a dime for every pipe I threaded. It was a neat job. I could work when I wanted, as long as I kept up with their needs. I could play when I wanted, as long as I didn't run out of money.

Soon enough the workers needed more pipe, and they hired a new kid. The new kid got fifteen cents a pipe. And they gave him an automatic threading machine. He made out like a bandit, while I got a measly nickel a thread.

It wasn't fair. It was better than fair (for the other boys). As for me, I realize now that I had plenty for myself. It was plenty before the other boys got the higher pay and it was plenty afterward. Both the parable of the Laborers in the Vineyard and the parable of the Two Sons are laden with "unfairness." But like my pipe threading job, it's all a matter of perspective. Whenever we compare our deserving to the deserving of others, our rewards never seem enough. But when we see how God provides what we need, we feel cared for abundantly. It's just that some receive more abundantly than others, but no one receives less than abundantly.

Is Justice Blind?

The two parables we've read raise questions about judgment. One brother says he won't go to work for his father and then does; the other says he will go to work and then doesn't. Both brothers fail in some fashion. Neither tells the truth in the beginning, but the better answer is the honest one, the answer of the first son who says up front he will not go, but then does. Why, though, when the chief priests and elders give the right answer does Jesus seem to reprimand them?

Jesus is quick to remind the temple authorities that they are not like the first son, lest they think the point of the story is to congratulate them on doing the will of their father. In essence, Jesus says that the temple leaders said no to one of their own in the beginning, and never changed their minds. They did not come to the vineyard later. The tax collectors and prostitutes, on the other hand, had no claim to Jesus in the first place, but they became Jesus' defenders when others distanced themselves from Jesus.

This parable reminds us a little of Nathan's parable for the good King David in 2 Samuel 12. David had committed adultery with Bathsheba, the wife of Uriah, one of David's fighting men. Nathan tells the parable of a rich man (David) who took a little ewe lamb (Bathsheba) from a poor man (Uriah). David quickly recognizes the wrongdoer in the parable, but he has to be told by Nathan that he is that man in real life. In the same way, the chief priests and elders give the right answer to the parable, but they do not correctly identify themselves in the story.

God was gracious with David: "Now the Lord has put away your sin; you shall not die" (2 Sam. 12:13). And God will be gracious with the chief priests and elders. They will not be banned from the kingdom of God, but neither will they be the first to enter. Those outsiders who heard and believed John the Baptist symbolize those who hear the gospel and believe it. They are the ones who will enter the kingdom of God first. As for the temple leaders, being last in the kingdom is a better outcome than the condemnation they may have deserved.

More Strange than Amazing.

Where the parable of the Two Sons is directed at Jewish leaders who participate in the judgment of Jesus, the parable of the Laborers in the Vineyard is directed to the insiders, the disciples. It comes just before the third passion prediction and just before two disciples ask Jesus if they can sit at his right and left hands in the kingdom of heaven. Apparently everyone wants to know what will happen to themselves in the judgment.

We're not all that surprised that outsiders (who become faithful) and Jewish leaders (people who should support Jesus but don't) will all receive grace in the end. Jesus ministers to outcasts (representing non-Jews), tax collectors (representing Jewish acquiescence to Roman rule), and prostitutes (sinners). The truly galling thing about the parable of the Laborers in the Vineyard is that Jesus is going to be gracious to latecomers. In fact, he will be more generous with those who come at the eleventh hour than with those who come early and stay all day.

If a "deathbed conversion" still gets us into heaven, why not fool around a bit while we're waiting? Wait a while before committing ourselves to the church; enjoy ourselves! Sure, accidents happen and we might die unexpectedly, but the risk is small and the "rewards" might just be worth the chance. What's the sense of living an intentionally righteous life if we can still get paid the full wage for working only the last hour of the day?

Dan Otto Via sums it up this way: "This surprising element [paying all the workers the same] woven into a realistic story suggests to us again that the divine dimension may cross our everyday reality to produce a crisis of ultimate importance in the midst of the ordinary. Our very existence depends upon whether we will accept God's gracious dealings, his dealings which shatter our calculations about how things ought to be ordered in the world."

If I Ruled the World . . .

Do you ever wonder how God makes judgments about people, what criteria God uses? Both parables tempt us to render a judgment about the characters and, by extension, about one another and ourselves. When we try, however, judgments aren't so clear-cut and easy to make. How do we judge the son who says yes right away, but who doesn't follow through? Does that not describe us? We profess to be Christians, but we often have feet of clay. Which one of us wants to offer ourselves up for condemnation?

We hit a similar snag in the parable of the Laborers in the Vineyard. Our sense of fairness is offended when the workers who come early and work all day seem to get shortchanged by the paymaster, but that's because we too quickly identify with the full-time workers. If we were to be honest, most if not all of us fall somewhat short of a full-time Christian. We work at it when it's convenient. We hang around the marketplace loafing when we don't have something better to do, so in the end, we don't want these people to be judged harshly. We are they.

Both of these parables appear only in Matthew's Gospel. Both are set in a narrative section that tells of the growing antagonism between Jesus and the powers that be. Matthew may have inserted the parable of the Laborers in the Vineyard into the narrative he borrowed from Mark as an illustration of the reversal of values in the coming kingdom. "But," as Norman Perrin says, "the parable fits that purpose uneasily, and it is an example of a parable . . . steadfastly resisting an attempt to serve a later and different context." That is to say it is more likely that Matthew includes it here to allude to some controversy in the first-century church, such as infighting between long term Christians and newcomers in the church. That's one reason it's difficult to understand the parable's meaning.

The parable of the Two Sons is unique to Matthew's Gospel, though it seems to be a shorter version of the parable of the Prodigal Son in Luke 15. As it's told in Matthew, it fits into the pre-passion story a bit better than the laborers in the vineyard, pointing up Matthew's emphasis on the failure of Jewish authorities to understand what or who the Messiah is.

However, the two sons do not fit so readily into Jesus' teaching on John the Baptist that immediately precedes the parable. If the father is John the Baptizer, who are the sons? The first son represents non-Jews who would have said no initially to John the Baptizer, but who changed their minds and became believers in his prophecy. But the second son does not represent anyone in particular. There is not a group who believed in the prophecy of John the Baptizer at first and later fell away. This suggests that the parable wasn't originally set in this context, even though Matthew probably found it that way in the narrative tradition upon which he drew in writing his Gospel.

An Uneasy Ambiguity

In both instances there's ambiguity. In both instances, we're left to wonder whose judgments are accepted and whose are rejected, who gets the Good Housekeeping Seal of Approval and who doesn't? It's finally not very satisfying to say that God can, after all, do what God wants. While it's true that God can do as God pleases, we like to think of God as a God of justice and reason.

Nor is it very comforting to know that God can surprise us. To be sure, God's actions in our lives may be surprising and unexpected. I don't want to minimize the wonder of that, but we like to think that God is a reliable God on whom we can count. When I studied the Hebrew Bible, the professor used to say that in the Hebrew Bible "God works in, through, and by means of the processes of time, space, and matter." He didn't mean to discount the extraordinary, but he did intend to locate the activity of God within the realm of human experience. God, who is in the processes of everyday life, can be counted on. But in many stories from the Hebrew Bible, there are hints of God's capriciousness; there is a little wonderment around the edges as to whether God has a plan or is just being arbitrary.

How should we regard God as seen through these two parables? Arbitrary? Unpredictable? Capricious? What should we think about our own judgment? In the New Testament, there's greater dependence upon the miraculous beyond the limits of time, space, and matter. Jesus' authority is reinforced by the many stories of healings, exorcisms, miracles, and more. Of course, the greatest of these stories is the resurrection, which certifies God's power over the forces of death. God remains, as God is in the Hebrew Bible, mysterious. God's ways are higher than our ways, God's thoughts deeper than our thoughts. We can never quite get a handle on God's intentions. And we are never quite comfortable with our understanding of what it is that God expects of us.

The good news is, according to the parables, that while God is unpredictable, God is never anything less than gracious. God may be unpredictably generous with those we least expect, but God is a God of grace for all of us—the self-inflated, the latecomer, and the halfhearted.

Interim Thinking

These questions again raise for me the fundamental point of all parables. The parables of Jesus never allow easy interpretation or application. There always remains a degree of uncertainty. Just when we think we've got it figured out, something happens to upset the apple cart. Just when we think we know what to do, something intervenes to press the question anew. Just when we think we've checked off all the right answers on the test that will get us into heaven, we're reminded that God grades the final exam. What good are our answers then?

I've worked with many interim ministers. Many are retired or semi-retired clergy who serve congregations in transition between pastoral calls. Some are intentional interims who serve troubled churches by helping them understand themselves and set goals before issuing a pastoral call. A few are what I call "unintentional interims" who walk into situations they don't expect and wind up moving on in relatively short order.

One of the wiser ministers I've worked with once commented, "All ministries are interim." Nobody stays anywhere forever. In that regard, the parables teach us that life itself is an interim. Nobody stays at the same level of faith all his or her life. Life is lived in the interim between creation and conclusion, and also in the interim between ambiguity and certainty. "For now I know in part, but, when that which is perfect has come, my knowledge will be complete" (author's translation of 1 Cor. 13:12).

If life is uncertain, we have two choices. We can throw up our hands and give up trying to understand it. Or we can roll up our sleeves and work with it. Which should it be?

Discussion and Action

1. In pairs, define or describe grace. Come back together and share your definitions. When you've arrived at some good definitions of grace, discuss whether grace is fair. Do the same with justice. Discuss how we ensure justice.

2. Make a list of occasions in which we judge others, such as grading school papers, making friends, and choosing employees. What makes a person qualified to judge others in these situations? Does a person have to be blameless to judge others? Why or why not?

3. Discuss this question: If you were God, what criteria would you use to judge who gets into heaven? How do the parables you've read help you?

4. Put yourselves in the parable of the Laborers in the Vineyard. Imagine that a timeline representing your life stretches across the room. One end is your birth, the other is now. Go and stand at the point at which you found faith. Look around you to see where everyone else is standing. How could you decide who is most deserving of heaven?

5. Which would be more impressive to God, the person who has been faithful for years, fending off temptation and sin, or the person who sinned badly but has used incredible inner strength to change? Why?

6. God is generous. Brainstorm ways to be generous in the coming week. Be ready to tell the group how you were generous and how it made you feel. For starters, pay a toll for the driver behind you, put an extra quarter in someone else's parking meter, give away something you treasure, make a treat for someone, support a charity, volunteer your time.

7. The disciples thought the final judgment would happen soon after Jesus' death and resurrection, but it didn't. Why don't people change, even when they've been given extra time? How genuine is change that is made at the last minute? How genuine is a lifelong faith that has not been tested?

8. Close by singing "Christian, let your burning light" on page 105.

8

Wicked Tenants and a Wedding Banquet

Matthew 21:33-44; 22:1-14

Faith is a response to God that is lived out in life.

Personal Preparation

1. Read Matthew 21:33–22:14. What image of God do you get from these parables? With which characters do you identify in each?
2. What fruit has your faith born? For instance, in what ways have you been obedient to the gospel in your personal life? How do you walk the talk?
3. In your mind or on paper, sketch out what you would like to say when sharing your faith. If you know someone who's considering becoming a Christian, how much should you tell them about the cost of discipleship? What is discouraging about the cost? What is encouraging?
4. Think about a wedding you have attended recently. What expectations are there of guests at a wedding? How is being a good wedding guest like being a faithful Christian?

Understanding

If you didn't see yourself as a culprit in the parable of the Laborers in the Vineyard or in the parable of the Two Sons, you will probably not escape judgment in the two parables for this session. There is a little bit of judgment for everyone in the parable of the Wicked Tenants and the parable of the Wedding Banquet. As Jesus spends his last days in Jerusalem, teaching about the end times and facing his own death, he first cautions individuals about how they will be judged in the end. But now he turns to talk about how God's people as a whole will be judged. The people who reject Jesus will lose the inheritance of the kingdom and the ones who have accepted him, that is the church, will receive it. But before we Christians become too complacent about our place in the kingdom, Jesus cautions that there is more to qualifying as a Christian than we may think.

Both of these parables are allegories. Each character in the parable equals a person in real life, and each event directly represents some actual event in history. Taken together, the two parables parallel the movement of God's salvation history from Abraham to the present, showing God's many attempts to relate to the people and save them, only to be rejected. We start out with the story of the wicked tenants. A landowner (God) plants a vineyard (the kingdom) and leases it to tenants (Israel) who are supposed to care for it and return a portion of the fruit to the landowner. However, when the landowner sends servants (the prophets) to remind the tenants of their obligation, the tenants kill the servants. Clearly, Jesus is referring to the numerous efforts of prophets in the history of Israel who tried to deliver God's message and each time were rejected. The first group of servants that the landowner sends represents the Former Prophets, and the second group of servants represents the Latter Prophets, which in Israelite history is the larger group, just as the second group of servants in the parable is larger than the first. Still they have no effect on the tenants.

As the parable goes, the landowner decides to send his son (Jesus), thinking that the tenants will respect the son more than the servants. Ironically, the tenants (Israel) see greater opportunity in killing this emissary (Jesus), because they stand to inherit the vineyard (the kingdom) if the landlord (God) has no heirs. It's dangerous to talk about Israel as a whole people here. It is really the temple leaders to whom Jesus is speaking and about whom he speaks. It's clear, however, that he's referring to what he knows is their desire to get Jesus out of the way. He's an irritant to them and the controller of their religious inheritance.

Notice how the tenants dispose of the landowner's son. "They seized him, threw him out of the vineyard, and killed him" (21:39). Isn't this a reference to the way that Jesus will die? He will be taken outside the wall of his spiritual home of Jerusalem as a *persona non grata* and killed like a common criminal. Little do the tenants know they cannot overcome the son ultimately. He will be the stone (which is a play on words with the word Son) that is rejected and becomes the cornerstone of a whole new movement.

All of this is to say, according to verses 43 and 44, that the ones who reject the gospel will not inherit the kingdom. Instead it will be handed over to those who accept the gospel and bear the fruits of righteousness because of it. This is the point at which Jesus is announcing that the church (that is, anyone who accepts the gospel) will become the bearers of the faith, God's chosen people.

Setting

With allegory there is a temptation to be too literal about equating roles and stories with real life people and events. In the parable of the Wicked Tenants, it is tempting to demonize all of Israel, attributing particular acts of unfaithfulness to every Israelite. The temptation to do so is heightened by the setting in which Matthew records the Gospel. Matthew wrote this Gospel around 80 A.D., in an era when the church was at terrific odds with Judaism. The temple in Jerusalem had been destroyed, Christians were no longer accepted as a Jewish group, and the church was undergoing a complete separation from its formerly Jewish identity. In retrospect, Matthew often portrays Jesus in conflict with Jewish authorities and is the only one of the Gospel writers to mention the church. Moreover, he pictures the church as a group set off from Judaism, something that didn't actually happen until long after Jesus. It's not surprising then that readers of Matthew tend to saddle all of Judaism with the shortcomings of its leaders and history.

Through a Glass Darkly

The chief priests and elders finally recognize themselves in the allegory and are furious. However, they can't silence Jesus because too many people see him as a prophet. This is an indication that they get his drift, but they themselves still do not accept him as a prophet and do not accept that his judgment is for them.

The temple leaders are not daft, at least no more daft than the rest of us. We all have trouble recognizing ourselves in the parables. In high school, I did a lot of drama. Once when I had the lead in a play, nothing seem to come together very well. The cast was large and the play was more complex than our usual productions. But the director was excellent, and our failure surely wasn't his fault.

The dress rehearsal was a disaster. The director lost his temper with the cast for not knowing their lines and mastering the blocking. We had stumbled through several scenes when he stopped us. He yelled at us for a few minutes—highly unusual for this mild-mannered man. Then he made us do it again and again. It got better. In fact, when the show opened, the performance went off pretty well, even if some of the cast were still learning their lines between scenes.

That was thirty years ago. About three years ago, one of my high school friends bombed me with the offhand comment that the director had been talking about me! I was the one he was yelling at for not learning my lines and knowing my blocking. Honest to goodness, I hadn't realized that in nearly thirty years.

By opening night, I knew all my lines. I knew my blocking and didn't trip over anybody. Why would he say that about me in particular? I guess what I hadn't learned was the fact that the play depended on my role. Since I had the lead part, all the other characters took their cues from my lines. They reacted to me; they played off my role. I had the responsibility of leading and I blew it, just as the temple authorities had blown it by not learning their lines and blocking regarding the kingdom of God. If I'm any example, it's not hard to go on for years denying our failures.

Wedding Feast

While the parable of the Wicked Tenants looks back to the history of God's saving acts and the rejection of the prophets, the parable of the Wedding Banquet looks to the future when the kingdom comes and the church takes up the banner of faith. This motion from the Old Testament to the New, from the nation Israel to the new nation (the church), distinguishes the two back-to-back judgment parables, but there is also an underlying sameness about them. The message that the servants (prophets) delivered to the tenants was not easy to hear or carry out, nor is the invitation that the servants offer to the wedding banquet guests.

A king (God) gives a wedding banquet (the messianic banquet ushering in the kingdom) for his son (Jesus). Servants (prophets or disciples) go out to invite the guests (invitation to receive the good news), but none of the guests come. Not only that, the invited guests mistreat the servants and kill them, which obviously infuriates the king. He has them done away with and burns their city (a reference to the destruction of Jerusalem), all while the roasted ox and the fabulous dinner wait. Then the slaves go out and bring in anyone they can find, good or bad, to fill the banquet hall.

Like the wicked tenants, the first wedding guests reject the message and the messengers. Who would refuse to go to a wedding feast on principle? In fact, Jesus uses a wedding feast in the parable because a wedding is cause for celebration and joy, something everyone can enjoy. You might think that a funeral dinner would be a better occasion to talk about judgment, but a wedding feast is used other places in scripture to symbolize the kingdom in which Jesus is the bridegroom and the church is the bride of Christ. So why would anyone refuse to come?

The parable says the invited guests make light of the offer (22:5). While we know that the pearl merchant and the farmer with the buried treasure were motivated out of exceeding joy and didn't mind selling all that they had for a greater joy, others, like the young man in Matthew 19:16-22, rejected Jesus' offer when they found out the cost of discipleship. Perhaps the wedding guests knew the costs that God's faithful had paid throughout history and thought that Jesus' invitation was foolish. And it is foolish in the world's terms.

I have to think back on my own wedding feast. I don't remember much about that day except a few little details. I remember that Jan forgot her veil. Just before the processional, her dad rushed home to get it and ran back just in time to put it on her head and walk her down the aisle. All the while, the rest of us were holding our breath and trying to smile. I think the organist improvised, playing the wedding processional more than once.

I remember that having an African American usher caused a little stir, too, not to mention the fact that I wore a beard when it was counter-cultural. And I remember the wedding guest book, which was a gift to us from a delightful older woman whose husband had been president of the college we were attending.

The thing I remember most, however, is that after the service, I got absorbed in an interesting conversation with the man who married us and another pastor. I was so engrossed in the discussion I missed my own wedding banquet. I guess I'm just like the first guests. Other things seemed more important at the time, like farm chores and business details. Whatever is most immediate and most pressing gets our attention, but not always the things that matter most.

The Replacements

When everyone else has rejected the invitation, the king sends servants, who play the same role that they played in the wicked tenants parable, to find more guests. The guests don't have to be any particular sorts of people; in fact they can even be bad people. They must only have received an invitation to get into the banquet. What good news for outcasts, sinners, and misfits! But then we find out that there is something the guests have to do in order to *stay* at the banquet. They have to conform to the "dress code."

We are used to seeing flip-flops in the social order in the Gospels. The blind can see, the poor are exalted, the lame can walk, the first will be last. So we're brought up a little short when a "friend" is cast out of the banquet for being improperly dressed. Doesn't Jesus want the humble and poor to be part of the kingdom? This is one of those places in the parables when we get tied up in knots if we try to be too literal. If we think of a wedding party (the kingdom) as a costly event (sell everything and give the money away), it's easier to see why the improperly dressed "friend" (unprepared guest) was cast out.

It's obvious that the guest is caught flat-footed by the notion: "He was speechless." He evidently had a certain level of understanding about what was required of him, namely attendance at the wedding. Knowing he was invited in a hurry and that the food was ready (the kingdom was prepared and waiting), it doesn't seem strange that he'd show up without proper attire. But it is also clear that his level of understanding about what was involved in accepting this invitation wasn't sufficient. This poor guest didn't know that he had to dress the part of a Christian as well as speak the part. He needed to live a kingdom life as well as assent to it. These two parables begin as a caution to Israel as it faces judgment and end with a caution to Christians who are no less susceptible to judgment. "Many are called, but few are chosen" (22:14).

In our zeal to spread the good news, we sometimes forget to tell the hard news. People get the notion that the only thing the Christian life requires of them is belief, of accepting the gift. Then they show up at church, amazed that still more is expected. It is true that there is nothing we can do to earn acceptance into God's realm, but it is also true that much is expected of us once we are.

In his book *The Parables*, Dan Otto Via says, "The man of Christian faith lives as one who is becoming, in between the radical offer of forgiveness and the demand for radical obedience— the essence of Jesus' message." It feels abrupt in the parable for the king to call the improperly clothed man "friend" and then throw him to the wolves. Our impulse is to give him a chance to become a disciple, but that is expecting too much from the parable. Jesus is only saying that faith is a response to God that is lived out in life. Anyone who assumes any less will not inherit the kingdom.

The idea of discipleship is present in the parable of the Wicked Tenants, too. Jesus notes at the end that the kingdom will be taken from the naysayer and given to those who bear fruit. Jesus is not suggesting that if people get busy doing good works they can escape judgment. Rather, the kingdom belongs to those who have faith and live it.

Troubling Stories

When we think literally about these parables, we're sometimes troubled by the image of God as a vengeful God. Will God "put those wretches to a miserable death"? Will God "destroy those murderers and burn their city"? It sounds drastic for the God who "saved a wretch like me." It is impossible to overstate the caution that these stories are parables and allegories. They are just as much about a loving God who tries over and over to offer grace as they are about damnation. They are about our folly as much as they are about God's breaking point. And they are as much about giving the kingdom to those who will bear fruit as they are about taking the kingdom away from those who don't want it anyway. It is not we who have suffered rejection nearly as much as it is God who has suffered rejection; yet God loves the recalcitrant people enough to keep trying. Grace is not cheap, but grace is always available whenever you and I want to take it and live it.

Discussion and Action

1. Through the parable of the Wicked Tenants, Jesus shows how God sent the prophets to the people over and over. Each one was rejected, even the Son of God. Who are the prophets of our day? What are they saying? Which messages are rejected? Which ones have people taken to heart?

2. In small groups or in the larger group, talk about what would happen if the judgment happened today. In what ways would you say you have been faithful? In what ways have you failed at being faithful?

3. The landowner has the tenants killed and the king has the invited guests killed? What, if any, is God's threshold for our disobedience?

4. What is a marriage made of? What must married people do, other than say vows, to really have a marriage? How is this like faith or life in the kingdom?

5. Work together to write a "dress code" for the kingdom. That is, what lifestyle do you have to "put on" in the kingdom? Look at Ephesians 6:10-17, for a sample. How well are the members of the covenant group clothed?

6. Look at pamphlets and membership materials for visitors and new members of your church. Critique it for how thoroughly it informs people of the cost of discipleship. Talk about whether the cost of discipleship should be mentioned up front, in stages, or after someone has been a member for a while? Which is best? Why?

7. Use colorful paper scraps or magazine clippings to design invitations. Invite people to become part of your congregation or covenant group. Send them to people you know who may be looking for a church home or who seem ready to begin a faith journey. It's not necessary to execute people who do not respond!

8. Close by singing "Here am I, Lord."

9

Bridesmaids and Talents: Signs of the Times
Matthew 25:1-30

If we live as decent citizens, but not as radical dis ciples, will Jesus recognize us as people of the kingdom?

Personal Preparation

1. Read Matthew 24 and 25 to give context to the two parables for this session. In what ways are you preparing for the end of your life? What shape are your relationships in? Are your affairs in order?

2. How much stock do you put in doomsday predictions? What's true about them for you? What is false? From you own vantage point, what does the long term future look like?

3. An old saw says that death and taxes are inevitable. Make your own list of the "inevitables" in your life. How do you make use of your time until the inevitable happens?

4. How many and what kind of risks are you willing to take in life? Do something risky this week, such as reaching out to an alienated friend, forgiving someone, or investing money in a project.

Understanding

Waiting for something that is both inevitable yet unpredictable is tough. My mom died of cancer. She struggled with it for more than six years. She had a mastectomy and a lengthy regimen of chemotherapy and radiation. The cancer returned and spread to her lung. She had more surgery and more therapy. Then the cancer returned again, this time in the brain. There wasn't much that could be done except to make her as comfortable as possible.

I've always wondered what she was thinking through it all. We talked about the disease and the future, but only briefly. She worked hard to keep up a brave face, and she succeeded wonderfully. In fact, I often think she was more help to us than we were to her.

The week of her death, I was in Arizona for meetings related to a new job I was just starting in Nebraska. I was supposed to move to Lincoln, Nebraska, while Jan and the kids stayed in Iowa until the school year ended. So I was separated from my family. I was disconnected from the congregation I had been serving. I hadn't yet gotten connected in the new community. I was in meetings with people I didn't know. And my mother's death was inevitable. I didn't know what to do except to keep doing.

I wondered at times if it made a difference that the waiting was long and drawn out. Do people make the most of the time before the end, putting things in order and getting relationships repaired? My mother must have known that death was close at hand, but what is close when pain and sickness linger? How do you get ready when all you seem capable of doing is to hold on?

Early on, my mother made a valiant effort to go about life as usual, as though she weren't sick. Some of that was an act, because she was really scared. We all were. Besides, nothing could ever be "usual" again Then there was a period when she focused only on the disease, especially during intensive treatment. She didn't do much other than struggle with it. And finally there was a time, as she approached the end, that she exuded a calm peace. But whether she was defying cancer, facing into it, or coming to terms with it, she was doing something with the news that the end was near.

She once told me that she had finally realized there were only two choices she could make about her cancer. She could either die from it, or she could live with it. She chose the latter. And that was, in the end, her victory over the accursed disease.

When Jesus walked out of the temple, the text says, he told his disciples that the destruction of the temple was inevitable. Not one stone in all these wondrous buildings would be left standing upon another. Then he launched into a lengthy discourse about the approaching end of the age, followed by three apocalyptic parables, two of which we'll look at in this session. Jesus sets out to do two things in this section: announce when the end will come (though he never fully tells) and what the faithful should be doing in the meantime.

The Little Apocalypse

Before we get to the parables of the end times, we need some background. The discourse in which the parables are found (Matt. 24–25) is an apocalyptic discourse, sometimes called the Little Apocalypse in contrast to the great apocalypses of Daniel and Revelation. Apocalyptic means *revealed*. The meaning of a mystery is revealed, God's plan is revealed, or, in this case, Jesus' return is revealed. The last book of the New Testament is an apocalypse (or revelation) to John that unveils the end of time and the return of Christ. Matthew, Mark, and Luke also devote a short section of each of their Gospels to an apocalypse of this same type.

More than a kind of writing, apocalypse is a way of thinking. Apocalyptic writers think in three ways: (1) that the worst of all possible outrages has just happened; (2) that God will intervene to set things right; and (3) that the faithful should hang on in the interim, despite persecution and hardship. In other words, apocalyptic writing is a way to encourage the saints who might otherwise despair, because apocalypse is not so much about the end of things or the loss of hope, as it is about the beginning of something new and the renewal of hope.

Apocalyptic writings flourished during a three-hundred-year period from 165 B.C. to 135 A.D. Judaism picked up this way of thinking and writing through the influence of the Persians, from whom Judaism borrowed many of its key images and ideas. But they didn't just pick up the apocalyptic style because they liked it. They experienced an "outrage" that must have seemed to them like the literal end of the world. In 165 B.C., the Seleucid ruler

Antiochus Epiphanes IV conquered Palestine and desecrated the temple. The Book of Daniel, especially the last seven or eight chapters, was written in the wake of this event, though the Daniel story is set much earlier in the period of the Babylonian exile. When the temple was reconsecrated in 163 B.C., the images and ideas of apocalyptic writing had made their lasting mark on Judaism.

Apocalyptic literature uses a standard stock of images and symbols, such as trumpets, wakefulness, and sleep, altering and adapting their application according to new circumstances. In the synoptic apocalypse, for example, the images and symbols come in a roundabout way from the last chapters of Daniel, roundabout because the Gospels borrowed them from the early Christian tradition of the first century, which had itself borrowed and adapted the material from Daniel.

Each of the Gospel writers recorded their account of Jesus' life and ministry decades after he lived. They weave incidences that happened after the resurrection back into the Gospel accounts as if they happened during Jesus' ministry. One of the monumental events of Matthew's life that gets worked back into Jesus' ministry is the destruction of the temple in 70 A.D. This event is the "outrage" that prompts Jesus to reveal the approach of the end times.

The so-called Little Apocalypse in Mark was written in the weeks immediately following the destruction of the temple. Matthew used Mark as the basis for his Gospel, but diminished the urgency of the Markan version, since Matthew wrote ten to twenty years later. Thus Matthew's version is longer and more drawn out, because Matthew assumed that the second coming had been delayed: "all these things must first take place," but "the end is not yet."

In Matthew's Gospel, the Little Apocalypse seems less concerned with when Jesus will return and more concerned with what the faithful should do in the meantime. His discourse becomes a teaching about the requirements of discipleship in the interim between the resurrection and the second coming, dwelling on the idea of readiness and offering instructions about what to do while we wait.

Be Prepared

Matthew doesn't dwell very long on the question of when the end will come. Mark, written at least ten years earlier, was certain the end was imminent, but Matthew attests that nothing happened in the next decade. He shifts the focus of the Gospel from naming a date for the end to Jesus' teachings on what to do in the interim. The parable of the Ten Bridesmaids is one of three stories about waiting and the consequences of not being prepared.

Ten bridesmaids go to wait for the bridegroom. They take their lamps, but only five of them take extra oil. Tired of waiting, the maids fall asleep until finally a shout goes up. The bridegroom is coming! But they have waited so long that the lamps have run out of the first oil. Five wise bridesmaids have more oil to fill their lamps. Five foolish bridesmaids must run to the market to get more oil. While they are away, the bridegroom arrives to join the five remaining maids and locks the door. When the shopping bridesmaids return, the bridegroom will not let them in and says he does not know them.

We're still dealing with parables of judgment, though the parables in chapter 25 are specifically about the moment of Christ's return and not just judgment in general. The problem is, how do we prepare for an event that is certain but unpredictable? The bridesmaids take their lamps, which in the Sermon on the Mount are symbols of good works and righteousness (Matt. 5:14-16), suggesting that we should all keep up the good works. But the women have to wait so long they become drowsy and fall asleep. Sleep is the state of inaction and shows up in apocalyptic literature as a symbol of unpreparedness. How can they be constantly prepared? How can they be alert at every moment?

It raises the question for us of the adequacy of our own preparation. All ten maidens seemed eager to do the right thing in the beginning, but all ten maidens, even the five wise ones, fell asleep. We have to sleep in order to be alert in the waking hours. But the fact that the foolish maidens didn't think of the future was what got them in trouble. They didn't think of the possibility that the end might be far off and that preparation meant being prepared

for the long haul. We are like them. We often have a lot of enthu-
siasm for a project in the short term, but as the time stretches out,
we become complacent. We tend to do good works only occasionally, and we lose the feeling that Christ's return is a sure thing.

It seems as if it's always the relatively simple mistake that costs
us so dearly. Like the foolish maidens, we are forgetful or halfhearted or complacent about our Christian discipleship. We're
not stingy or mean-spirited, but without a deadline or a sense of
urgency, we drift along in a dream world, not thinking about the
gospel. When the foolish bridesmaids return with more oil, the
bridegroom (Jesus) doesn't recognize them. They have neglected
their descipleship until they look like everyone else in the world.
If Jesus recognizes Christians by their obedience to the gospel,
will Jesus recognize us? If we're living as decent citizens, but not
as radical disciples, will Jesus recognize us as people of the
kingdom? It's a minor distinction in our culture, but it has
huge consequences.

Remember that the wedding guest was sent out because he
was improperly dressed. He did not look like a disciple. He didn't
do the things that a true believer would do, such as good works,
so the king didn't recognize him as an insider. Belief and eagerness are not enough for wedding guests or bridesmaids.

Make Hay

The parable of the Talents is also about preparing for the end
times. A man entrusts his fortune to several men while he is away.
The first man receives five talents, which he invests, and doubles
the amount. The second man receives two talents and also doubles
his amount. The third man, fearful of the master's judgment, bur-
ies a single talent, digs it up, and returns it to the lender when he
returns from his trip. The master appreciates the efforts of the
first two to care for the money, but he chastises the third man for
failing to make anything of the money in his possession and throws
him into the "outer darkness."

This allegorical parable is much like the parable of the Ten
Bridesmaids, some of whom are foolish and some of whom are
wise. The characters here have various abilities. One is a very

successful businessman. One is very good businessman. And one is no businessman at all. It doesn't seem to matter to the master what degree of success the men have, only that they work hard to do something with the money. The third man does nothing and that's the problem.

Apparently the third man is suspicious of the master. He thinks the master is a harsh man, "reaping where you did not sow, and gathering where you did not scatter seed" (25:24). He even confesses to being afraid of the master, so much so that when he received his talent, he went into a mode of self-preservation, doing only what he thought would not put him at risk. Taking no risk, however, puts him at the greatest risk ever.

By its very definition, faith takes risks, and a life of faith is a life of constant and daily risk. What could be more risky than extending love and forgiveness, of offering service, eating with outcasts, and turning the other cheek? These are not activities that a Christian does in the meantime, but the things a Christian does all the time as a lifestyle of faith. Just because the end is at hand and the time is uncertain does not mean we should stop doing these things and wait. Jesus would say, "Keep on."

Some have remarked that the kingdom is "already but not yet." That is, it's both in the future and, insofar as we make it, it is in the present. To stop living in obedience to the gospel is to deny that Jesus has already brought part of the kingdom in.

After Jesus' resurrection, Acts records that he appeared many times to the disciples and finally ordered them to go to Jerusalem and wait for him there. They want to know if Jesus will return to them once and for all in Jerusalem and if he will restore the kingdom to Israel. God tells them, "It is not for you to know the times or periods that the Father has set by his own authority" (Acts 1:7). Then he tells them what to do in the meantime. Work. Go to the ends of the earth as witnesses for Jesus Christ. And so they do.

Our impulse is to look toward the end of time as a relief from this world of toil. We want to look at the end as a reward for an earthly life of obedience, a reward of rest and relaxation. But the kingdom is one of those surprising places. The reward is not rest but joy. Everything is costly, but no one minds paying. And small, insignificant things according to the world, like the gospel, become great. The kingdom is full of the unexpected reversals.

I think I experienced one of those kingdom reversals when my mother died. At the last, I wasn't prepared for her to go. It was wrenching and disconcerting. It upset everything I had come to count on, and it put a hole in my hope. Then, at the funeral as she had requested, the congregation sang "Love lifted me." And I remembered her saying that she could choose to die from cancer or choose to live with it. That alone was enough to put a patch over the hole in my hope.

Discussion and Action

1. What have you done as you've waited for something important, such as the results of a medical test, the birth of a baby, news of a promotion at work, or acceptance into college? How would you rate the quality of your patience when you wait?

2. How do you tend to think of the end of your life? As something far off or just around the corner? What effect does that have on the way you live your life?

3. What signs, if any, do you see in culture or nature that things are coming to an end? What is your contemporary equivalent of the "desolating sacrilege"?

4. Make doomsday predictions. From your vantage point, how will the world end? When will it happen? Who are the doomsday pundits of our time? What is compelling about their predictions? What is unbelievable?

5. Share some of the ways you have prepared for the end of your life. At about what age do people begin to think about preparing for the end? How much are they motivated by fear and judgment? How much are they motivated by joy of living in obedience to the gospel? How could young people be convinced that faith and discipleship are joys and not duties.

6. In what way is faith an act of self-preservation for you? In what way is faith a risk? What risks are you willing to

take for faith? Which ones have you already taken? Write your name on an index card. Pass your card to each member of the group and ask each person to write a challenge on your card. Do the same for others as their cards come around the circle.

7. Have a "Talents Contest" in your congregation or group. Have each member take an amount of money and, over a period of time, make it multiply. Be creative and see what happens! Give the income to your congregation or to your favorite mission.

   Another version of this is to "play the stock market." Pretend to invest money ($1000) in stocks or commodities. Keep track of the "investments" over a period of time. Discuss what happened to your money, and discuss why you made your investment choices.

8. Close by singing "Joy to the world."

10

The Sheep and the Goats
Matthew 25:31-46

A decision for faith delivers us into a life lived automatically according to the gospel.

Personal Preparation

1. Read Matthew 25:31-46. Based just on good works, how would you fare in Jesus' eyes? How would the non-Christians you know fare in Jesus' eyes based on good deeds? How do you believe Jesus relates to non-Christians?

2. In ancient Hebrew culture, people were to receive emissaries as if they were the very person they represented. How well or poorly are you able to receive all representatives of Christ as if they were he? What can you do for the poor and the prisoner if they are Christ's emissaries?

3. After ten weeks of studying the kingdom of God, how has your vision of the kingdom changed? remained the same? How, if at all, has it changed the way you feel you should live your life?

4. If you were describing the Gospel according to Matthew to a stranger, what would you say in a nutshell?

Understanding

Johnny Carson not only made a career of explaining his jokes. When asked what he'd like to do, he once commented that he wanted to be a shepherd. The idea of sitting on a hillside, tending sheep, watching the dog, and maybe playing a pan flute really appealed to him. Some days, I have to admit, it sounds pretty good to me too!

Better a shepherd than a sheep, though, and better a sheep than a goat, according to Matthew. Goats do not fare very well in the parable of the Sheep and the Goats. They are saddled with the unfortunate stigma of representing pagans and nonbelievers. Like a lot of phrases in the Bible, Matthew's characterization of good people as sheep and bad people as goats has made its way into our everyday speech, but not without some reason. Apparently sheep were more valuable than goats in the economy of Jesus' day.

Matthew 25:31-46 is an apocalyptic passage, complete with signs, such as the coming of the Son of Man in glory, judgment, and a gathering of the nations. While we sometimes refer to it as a parable, only the few verses about the shepherd separating the sheep and the goats is an allegorical parable, perhaps taken from a longer parable of another time. The rest of the passage is a description of how Jesus will judge who's in and who's out of the kingdom in the end times.

Sheep to the Right, Goats to the Left

Christ will be as a shepherd who separates the sheep and the goats, putting sheep on the right and goats on the left. To the sheep he will say, the kingdom is for you, because you cared for me when I was thirsty, hungry, sick, and in prison. The sheep, not remembering their good work, will ask the Shepherd when they did these things. The Shepherd will respond that when they did it to the least and the lowly, they did it to him by extension. To the goats he will say, you will be damned because you did not care for me when I was thirsty, hungry, sick, and in prison. The goats, not remembering any such failure, will ask when they ignored him. The Shepherd, irked by their carelessness and ignorance, will say they did not care for others, and so they did not care for him.

This passage has been used countless ways. Some have used it to condemn people of other faiths. Others have used it to defend the worth of people who do not profess Christianity, but who behave as Christians. It has been used to limit Christian service to

Christians (the least of "my family") only, and it's been used to expand Christian service to outsiders. It's been used to support the idea that the kingdom is in the immediate future, and it's been used to say that the kingdom is present now and has been present since "the foundation of the world" (25:34). I want to ask three questions about this text to help us see what it might be saying: What does the text tell us? What's *not* there? What are we supposed to do in reaction?

What Does the Text Tell Us?

Without a doubt, this section of Matthew's Gospel tells us that entry into the kingdom is based on how we relate to other human beings. When people feed the hungry, clothe the naked, visit the sick, and stand with the prisoner, they are living as disciples, doing as Jesus would do. What's more, if they do these things to the least and the lowly, they have done them to Jesus himself. It was customary in Jewish thought to believe that a person's emissary deserved all the respect and authority of the person represented. If people are truly followers of Christ, they go to the hungry, the thirsty, the sick, and the prisoner as if Christ himself goes. But if they do not go in Christ's name, they can have no part of him.

Notice that the faithful are surprised to find out they have done all this. They want to know when they have done these things for Jesus. Surely we know when we've done good deeds, but do we? When we're disciplined to be polite, are we aware we're doing it? When we're accustomed to deferring to others or always watching out for someone weaker or needier, are we always aware? A decision for faith delivers us into a life lived automatically according to the gospel. How can one live authentically any other way? If that's so, then the faithful would not recognize anything unusual about doing the work of Jesus. It took a blessing from Jesus to jog their memories.

Poverty Up Close

As Christians (wealthy Christians, actually, by the world's standards), we can assume that there is hunger and need anywhere, anytime. While most of the hunger we see is on the far side of the globe, and then only do we see it by way of television and newspapers, there is probably hunger and need very close at hand. There may be people who are hungry in our own congregations, people who sit next to us in the pew on Sunday morning. Often, the elderly don't eat well. I once discovered that an elderly couple in my congregation was eating canned dog food because they couldn't afford meat. Some children don't eat well because their single parent is working at minimum wage just to pay the rent.

The woman in the thin coat isn't naked, but she might not be able to afford a warmer coat for winter. The older man who always wears the same shirt may not have another one. Holes in some child's tennis shoes may not be a fashion statement, but a statement of need.

While we often miss opportunity to serve the poor and needy, we may also be blind to the number of people who are quietly ministering to others. There's a woman I know who lives in a small town south of my home. She was a member of the congregation I served there. Only after she left the community three years later did I find out that for more than thirty years she had been driving a great distance to visit convicts in a state prison. She corresponded with them regularly, visited at least monthly, and kept in touch with them when they were released. She never said a word about it. Her daughter mentioned it offhandedly one day. I was surprised, but I shouldn't have been; it was a natural part of her Christianity.

Making a Difference

Most of us will never know what a difference we make in the lives around us. We're lucky if we discover it, unless the accolades spoil our modesty. Most of the time I think we're really a little flattered, but we like to pass off compliments as exaggeration or a mistake. I once taught a New Testament course at a university. I usually thought I'd done a decent job and I got good evaluations from most of the students. One day a student named Jeff knocked on my door just after the fall term ended. I thought he wanted to know his grade on the final exam. Instead, I was surprised to learn that he had a present for me. I'm not in the habit of accepting presents from students, but the grades were already turned in and the term was finished. Besides, it was Christmas time and he was so sincere. I opened the package to find a wonderful pen and ink drawing of a small waterfall scene somewhere in rural Pennsylvania. He'd signed and dated it for me. It was lovely.

The real gift, however, came when Jeff told me that after his encounter with the New Testament in my class he had decided to pursue a career illustrating religious books. For all I knew, he may have had other reasons, but I was still deeply flattered. The Spirit probably had more to do with it than anyone, but the New Testament course seemed to be the catalyst. I simply wasn't aware that I'd had such an influence on him.

What *Isn't* Said

In the *Interpretation* commentary (Matthew), Bible scholar Douglas Hare points out that there is nothing particularly Christian about the story of the sheep and the goats. Good works do not distinguish it as a Christian teaching, since other religions and cultures also believed that good behavior would be rewarded in the afterlife. It's noticeable that Jesus doesn't say entrance into the kingdom depends on right belief, though that's clearly important in the rest of the Gospel. He doesn't say that it depends on right doctrine, though one of Matthew's major concerns is helping the young church establish a doctrinal tradition. He doesn't say that it depends on going to church every Sunday, though Matthew certainly values the fellowship of the faithful. He doesn't say that it depends on being baptized, although the Great Commission a few chapters later is a ringing endorsement of baptism. None of the usual marks of membership are mentioned.

Those who would use this passage to discriminate against people of other religions are standing on thin ice. When I was growing up, there was a lot of anti-Catholic sentiment. I recall hearing it from the pulpit in the little church we attended for a while, and I remember hearing it often from my friends. Some of you may remember that the dangers of Roman Catholicism were a hot topic in the 1960 presidential election. I even recall voting for Nixon in a mock election because of it: A Catholic in the White House? Never!

The issue wasn't whether I had Catholic friends; I had lots. I had remarkably few prejudices with regard to race or ethnicity, probably because of my upbringing. But there was something about the Catholic-Protestant divide that was an unbridgeable gulf. When I was twelve, I even trudged across the backyard toting my Bible to have a debate with Jimmy LaRock, a Catholic neighbor. He trounced me.

So What Are We to Do?

The day my dad left the church turned things around for me. With no Disciples congregation nearby, we had joined a small independent congregation in a nearby town. My dad was president of the men's fellowship and had arranged a program on alcoholism. When the evening was over, some of the men told him that if he ever did anything like that again, he needn't come back.

It wasn't the subject matter they objected to; it was touchy but not taboo. It wasn't the presentation; it was quite good. It wasn't the presenter's credentials; he was a trained and certified counselor, and a pastor at that. The problem was the presenter was Lutheran!

My dad was so angry and hurt that he left the church. It took him and the rest of the family years before we found a new church home. Imagine the Shepherd separating the Catholics from the Protestants and the Methodists from the Presbyterians. Where would it all end? In retrospect, it seems so silly. The anti-Catholic stuff was one thing, but prejudices against a Lutheran? in Minnesota?

Without a doubt, that incident has shaped me to a great extent. It's why I value the ecumenical tradition so deeply. I can argue with my friend, the Catholic bishop; and I can get frustrated with the ethnic exclusivity of the Lutherans; and I can have sharp differences with my Baptist friends—but I just can't assign any of them so easily to the left hand with the goats, the outsiders of the kingdom.

What finally counts for me, as well as for this section of Matthew's Gospel, is how faithful we are. And faith is shown in action not because works save us, but because the faithful can do no other. The ethics of kingdom living are a natural and inevitable reaction to the Gospel.

I'm using the word *reaction* deliberately, because I think the word *response* carries with it a sense of doing "this for that." God acts and we respond. But a reaction is literally a re-action. Matthew's theological point is that God has acted in Jesus Christ decisively and definitively to alter the course of human history. To re-act this act of God is to imitate the action of Christ: inasmuch as you have done it for the least of these, you have done it for me.

Shaking Things Up

The greatness of the gospel tradition is that it enables us to re-act the act of God in Christ Jesus. The parables not only give us clarity about the questions that face us as human beings trying to live as Christ lived, they also turn the world upside down, forcing us to examine and reexamine all of the assumptions we have about the way life should be lived. They force us to make and remake our decisions in each and every moment of our living. They force us to pay attention.

We only need to rehearse the titles. The Mustard Seed. The Treasure in the Field. The Sower. The Unforgiving Servant. The Lost Sheep. The Talents. All indelible in our memories. All bring to mind countless connections to real life. All clarify the kingdom. Every one a question. Every one a statement of hope. Every one disconcerting. All simple stories. Every one complex.

"Whoever can give his people better stories than the ones they live in is like the priest in whose hands common bread and wine become capable of feeding the very soul" (Kenner, *The Pound Era*).

Discussion and Action

1. If you were dividing the sheep and the goats for the kingdom, what criteria would you use? How does your system differ from that of Jesus? How is it the same?

2. How do you think non-Christians will be judged?
3. Spend a few minutes in silence, forming a doctrinal statement in your mind. In other words, say what you believe about God and Jesus in no more than a few sentences. Then take turns stating, if you wish, your personal "doctrine" of faith. In your belief, is belief or action more important? Why?
4. Tell each other stories of encounters you have had with prejudice against other Christians or people of other faiths. Brainstorm some reactions that you could use next time you witness such prejudice.
5. In what ways do you behave automatically as a Christian? To what extent is this behavior instinctual and natu ral? To what extent is it learned by training and discipline? What can we do to instill Christian behavior in children, young people, and adults? Is this happening in your congregation? How could it happen more often?
6. What new insights do you have into the parables? How much did the parables clarify your vision of the kingdom of God? How much did they raise questions? What questions did the parables raise for you? Talk about these questions as a group. What clarity can you give each other?
7. Fill in the blanks.
   The kingdom of God is like

   _____

   God is like

   _____

   God's judgment is like

   _____

   The end of time will be like

   _____

   Consider recording the responses in writing, on an audiocassette, or on video tape. Share these responses with the congregation through the newsletter or in worship.
8. Close by again singing "Tell me the stories of Jesus."

Suggestions for Sharing and Prayer

We use parables almost without knowing it. When we try to describe an indescribable experience, we use parable. When we try to teach our children lessons, we use parables. When we try to understand the world in which we live, we think in parables. Sometimes parables make sense of the nonsensical. Sometimes parables help us understand with some other part of our being than the mind. Sharing and Prayer will help you practice the art of thinking in and teaching in parables.

In addition to the ideas for prayer and sharing listed here, consult the scriptural allusion index and topical index in your hymnal or songbook for more music. Read, sing, or pray them. Use them as litany, confession, and praise. Also, incorporate the discipline of writing or creating parables into your gatherings and between gatherings. Reserve time in each meeting to share what you've created. Collect copies of each person's parables into a booklet or folder and make them available to the editor of your church newsletter and your pastor who might like to use them for worship.

Doug Bland, author of these Suggestions for Sharing and Prayer, is pastor of Community Christian Church in Tempe, Arizona.

1. The Mustard Seed

❏ In a book called *The Pound Era*, Hugh Kenner says, "Whoever can give his people better stories than the ones they live in is like the priest in whose hands common bread and wine become capable of feeding the very soul." Who have been the important storytellers in your life? Parents? Grandparents? Neighbors? Pastors? Teachers? Others? Repeat some of the stories that have "fed your soul."

❑ As you study parables about tiny seeds, get to know each other better with the help of some big seeds—peanuts! Take five or six peanuts in the hull. For every peanut you may ask any question you want and receive an answer from your partner.

1. Stand up and find someone you would like to get to know better.
2. Break open the peanut shell and offer your partner your question and a peanut. After your partner answers, he or she may eat the peanut. Having heard his or her answer, you may eat one of your partner's peanuts. Now you are "Peanut Partners."
3. Switch partners every 30 seconds until all the peanuts are gone.

❑ Good poems and stories spark associations in our imaginations and help us make connections between the stories and our own lives. Read, for example, William Carlos Williams' poem "The Red Wheelbarrow" from a poetry collection. What memories or images does it bring to mind? Or focus on a simple object, such as a shovel, iron, or a piece of fruit.

Spend time in quiet. If you feel called, share aloud what you think of when you hear the parable of the Mustard Seed. What places do you travel in your imagination? What experiences do you associate with the parable?

❑ Where in your life or the life of your congregation have you seen "yeast power" (something hidden) or the "mustard seed influence" (something small) having a big impact? Write a letter of thanks to an unsung hero who has made an important contribution to your life.

❑ Dan Davis says that the word *parable* is a red cap word—it carries a lot of baggage. What other words are important enough to you that you would say they "carry a lot of baggage"? On a scale of one bag to ten bags, how many bags would you assign the following words:

Health	1	2	3	4	5	6	7	8	9	10
Hope	1	2	3	4	5	6	7	8	9	10
Belonging	1	2	3	4	5	6	7	8	9	10
Love	1	2	3	4	5	6	7	8	9	10
Family	1	2	3	4	5	6	7	8	9	10
Home	1	2	3	4	5	6	7	8	9	10
Truth	1	2	3	4	5	6	7	8	9	10
Church	1	2	3	4	5	6	7	8	9	10

Compare your answers with others. Add more words to the list. Talk as a group about what baggage each word carries.

2. Three Simple Parables: Yeast, Treasure, Pearl

❑ Make a name tag for yourself that illustrates what your name means. Then tell the group the story of your name. Perhaps you know the meaning or the nationality of your name. Why did your parents choose your name? Recall a humorous, interesting, or poignant incident associated with your name? Where is a safe and welcoming place where "everybody knows your name" and loves you nonetheless?

❑ In the parables of the Treasure and the Pearl of Great Value, those who find them go and sell everything in order to obtain the valued treasure. Perhaps you can think of some Christians who have given up much for the sake of the gospel, which they treasured more highly than anything else (for example: St. Francis, Martin Luther King, Jr., Mother Teresa). Tell their stories. Do you know of others closer to home?

❑ Speaking of treasures, what are some of your most treasured possessions? If there was a fire in your home and you could save only three things from destruction, what would you save? Could you sell these things if your faith depended on it? Why or why not? Have a mock garage sale. Name a favorite possession on an index card. Pass your card around and let those who would like to have it name a price they would be willing to pay. Talk afterward about whether it would be worth selling the item for the price offered.

❑ In our culture we put a great deal of emphasis on the rights of the individual and "private property." We speak of *my* car, *my* house, *my* stereo, *my* clothes. Consider an alternative point of view. Pray the words of the fourth-century church father Basil the Great:

When someone steals a man's clothes
    we call him a thief.
Should we not give the same name
    to one who could clothe the naked
    and does not?
The bread in your cupboard
    belongs to the hungry man;
the coat hanging unused
    in your closet
belongs to the man
    who has no shoes;
the money which you
hoard up
    belongs to the poor.

❑ Make up a parable that will help us experience one or more of these well-known maxims:

1. "An ounce of prevention is worth a pound of cure."
2. "A bird in the hand is worth two in the bush."
3. "A stitch in time saves nine."
4. "Out of sight, out of mind."
5. "Absence makes the heart grow fonder."

3. The Sower and the Seed

❑ Think back upon your life in terms of the four kinds of soil described in the parable of the Sower. What periods of your life would you identify as being "good soil" (where a bountiful crop was produced)? What period of your life was "rocky" (without much soil, plants grew and withered in the hot sun)? When have you experienced seeds falling on "the path" (where the birds came and ate up the seed)? Have you ever experienced "thorns" (that grew up and choked the plants just as they were getting started)?

❑ People often say that they don't have stories to tell, but sometimes asking the right question will access stories we don't even know we have inside us. Try these prompts:

1. Can you remember a time when you broke something that belonged to someone else?
2. Can you remember a night your parents never found out about?
3. Can you remember a birthday or holiday you would (or would not) like to live over again?
4. Can you remember a time when you got locked out of where you needed to be?
5. Can you remember a time when something you cooked didn't work out?

❑ Matthew and Mark seem to have different understandings of the role of parables. As the author of this study suggests, Mark tells us that Jesus used parables *in order* that listeners might see but not perceive and hear but not understand (Mark 4:10-12). Matthew says that Jesus told parables *because* listeners see without perceiving and hear without understanding (Matt. 13:13,14; 35). For Mark, the parables were strange riddles intended to *conceal*. For Matthew, the parables were stories intended to *reveal*.

What parables or stories have you used to conceal a sensitive issue from children, such as sex or death? What parables or stories have helped you reveal other basic truths to children?

❑ It is said that powerful stories have two qualities. First, they help us recognize ourselves in them. We can identify with them saying, "Yes, I know what it is like to be there, to experience that." Second, they are different enough from us to stretch us or call us beyond ourselves. How is the parable of the Sower similar to your life experience? How does it stretch you in some new ways?

❑ Place a concept in the middle of a page, then, individually or in small groups, jot down a dozen or so words which immediately come to mind. Here is an example:

Jesus Christ

Sacrament   Disciples

God   LORD'S SUPPER   Bread

Last Supper   Covenant

Upper room   Faith

Wine   Love

Cross

Such clustering can be used to help people think through their own understandings of an idea. The starting word might also be *parable, seed, story, Jesus*, etc.

4. Weeds, Wheat, and Fishnet

❑ A Jewish *midrash* (story based on scripture) tells us:

One day Abraham invited a beggar to his tent for a meal.When grace was being said, the man began to curse God, declaring he could not bear to hear His name. Seized with indignation, Abraham drove the blasphemer away.

Interrupt the story at this point to discuss whether Abraham should have driven him away. The man was, after all, "a bad fish," a real "weed." Was Abraham justified in his actions? After discussing these questions, continue with the story:

When Abraham was at his prayers that night, God said to him, "This man has cursed and reviled me for fifty years and yet I have given him food to eat every day. Could you not put up with him for a single meal?"

How is this story like the parables about the weeds and the bad fish? Of the three stories, which do you relate to most easily? Why?

❏   Without naming names, are there "good fish and bad fish," "wheat and weeds" in your congregation? Mine too. Billy Graham once said, "If you ever find a perfect church, don't join it. You'll ruin it." What do you think he meant by that? What does this say about God's patience? human accountability? Are there limits to this grace-filled attitude of tolerance? Has there ever been a time when you thought it was important to "do some weeding" because the whole harvest was threatened?

❏   In a children's sermon, the pastor asked the children of the church a question: "If all the good people of the world were purple and all the bad people of the world were green, what color would you be?" One little girl was courageous enough to answer with honesty. "Striped," she said.

What color would you be? Would there be anyone who would not be striped? How much sin will God tolerate, do you think?

❏   In his parables, Jesus shows an extraordinary ability to see the holy in ordinary, everyday objects. The following is an exercise in seeing the extraordinary in the ordinary. Take a square piece of aluminum foil and wad it up loosely into a random shape. Use your imagination. What does the shape look like? A mountain? A lion? A football? A spaceship? Tell the group what your foil wad represents.

❏   Retell the biblical story. Give someone in the group a ball of yarn and ask him or her to begin the story like this: "Once there was a garden paradise called Eden. In this garden . . ." The first person provides a few details in a sentence or two and then passes the ball on to someone across the circle. The next person adds a few more details, passes the ball on, and so on. Don't feel you need to tell the story straight from the "authorized version" with every jot and tittle correct. Use your imagination. Continue passing the ball until everyone has had at least one chance to speak and the story is told. You will have created a story web in the middle of the circle.

5. The Seeking Shepherd and the Lost Sheep

❑ Encourage group support. Invite the group to respond to the following question: What can each of us do to make others feel more comfortable and free to respond in group discussion? List these ideas on newsprint and tape it to the wall where your group meets.

❑ Pair off with one other person. Ask three times, Who are you? Give your partner the opportunity to give a different answer each time the question is asked. Trade roles and repeat the question.

Next, ask three times, Who are you becoming? Answer three times in different ways. Again trade roles.

Then introduce each other to the larger group based on what you learned in the interviews.

❑ How does your church family handle conflict? Who would you talk to about seeking a resolution? Look together at your bylaws or constitution for procedures for resolving conflict.

Here is a three-step procedure for dealing with complaints you might have in your congregation, family, or place of work.

1. Listen with compassion to the concerns being voiced.
2. In suggesting that the person with the complaint go directly to the "problem person," ask:
   a. Have you spoken to [*the problem person*]?
   b. May I go with you to [*the problem person*]?
   c. May I tell [*the problem person*] that you have this concern?
3. Let those with complaints know that you will not continue to listen to their concerns if they are not willing to seek constructive solutions.

In what real or imagined cases could this method be used? How does it differ from Matthew 18? What, if anything, keeps you from using a method like this?

❑   *Parable*. The word comes from two Greek words: *para* meaning "along side"; *bolo* meaning "to throw." Parables, then,
are stories that Jesus "throws along side" of our lives to help
us gain new insights and experience life at a deep level. What
happens when you hear the parable of the Lost Sheep "along
side" of your life? What images are strongest for you? What
connections can you make between your life and the parable?
What would you like to say to the lost sheep? to the shepherd? to the ninety-nine?

❑   The scripture for this session comes down hard on anyone
who "puts a stumbling block before one of these little ones."
They will get a large millstone hung around their neck and be
thrown into the sea. On the other hand, Jesus says that whoever welcomes a little child in his name welcomes him.

What characteristics of children are also characteristics of
Christians? Spend time in prayer, praying aloud the prayers
you prayed as children. Pause between each one to meditate
on it.

6. The Unforgiving Servant

A bumper sticker reads "I owe, I owe, so off to work I go."
That could describe a lot of us. To whom are you in debt? for
money? for love? for forgiveness? for an opportunity or break?
Make out IOUs in the form of greeting cards for people in all
these categories. Let them know how indebted you are and
how grateful.

As you're working, talk about what's good about being in
debt to one another? Also, talk about balance. Does it seem
as if you are always in debt or that people are indebted to
you? How does it feel on both ends of that equation? What is
the difference, if any, in the way you relate to creditors and
debtors?

❑   What's the difference between trespasses and debts in the various ways we say the Lord's Prayer? Make a list of your tres-

passes and another list of debts. In silent prayer, concentrate on each one, asking forgiveness.

❏ C. H. Dodd, author of *The Parables of the Kingdom*, defines parable as "an extended metaphor or simile drawn from nature of the common life, arresting the hearers by its vividness or strangeness and leaving the mind in sufficient doubt about its precise application as to tease the hearer into active thought." Why do you think Jesus would go to such lengths to tease the hearer? Why didn't he just come out and say what needed to be said?

❏ Both a metaphor and a simile are figures of speech that compare one thing with another. A simile uses "like" or "as" to make comparison. For example, "Rattlesnake tastes like chicken." Make up some similes by completing the following sentences:

as cold as _____

as hot as _____

as mean as _____

he runs like _____

her kisses are like _____

Metaphor makes a comparison by putting two things together that usually don't belong together; a metaphor does not use *like* or *as*. For example, "unfriendly sky," "good Samaritan," "the ship plows the sea."

Create a metaphor to describe the Bible; for example, "The Bible is the rock on which we stand" or "Jesus' parables are ants in the pants of faith." Create some metaphors to describe prayer, hope, Jesus, faith, and the kingdom.

7. Hard Messages: The Laborers in the Vineyard

❏ Some would say that parables run counter to logic. Offer definitions of logic. Give an example of a parable that you think uses good logic. Give an example of a parable that you think uses poor logic. To what degree should Christians rely on logic?

❑   Sometimes words wear out. Even really important words, such as *righteousness, forgiveness, sin,* and *love,* lose their meaning when they are used too much. Jesus' solution was to see God at work in ordinary, everyday objects and people—tiny seeds, sweaty workers, bread rising, alienated brothers. Look around you. Take a few minutes to find an ordinary object. Bring it to a place where the group can focus on it. Begin praying about the term *righteousness,* looking for ways that the gathered objects represent righteousness. Then shift to forgiveness. After a few minutes, shift to sin. Finally, focus on love.

❑   Identical wages are given to both early and late workers. What does that say to you about God's grace?

❑   Who works harder? Professional athletes? Mothers of young children? Attorneys? High school teachers? Preachers? Accountants? Police? Stockbrokers? Street sweepers? Carpenters? Artists? Engineers? If you were making out the paychecks, working with a salary cap of $100,000, what would you pay these people commensurate with the value of their work to society? In how many cases did you pay more than the actual salary these people make?

❑   The two sons surprise us by their responses to their father. Are you a good judge of character? Have you ever been fooled by someone's outward demeanor? Tell stories of people who surprised you—pleasantly or otherwise. Which son's story is most similar to your own? How so?

❑   The two sons in this parable are interesting character studies. The first is honest; the second says what he thinks his father wants to hear. Spend time in prayer being honest with God. If you feel called, complete the sentence prayer aloud: "Lord, to be really honest, I . . ."

8. Wicked Tenants and a Wedding Banquet

❑ Play out this image. Jesus likens the kingdom of God to a great wedding banquet. But after the banquet is the marriage. How is the kingdom like marriage?

Read wedding vows in unison from a pastor's manual as a covenant for the group.

❑ Jesus suggests that every time we gather around the table we get a foretaste of the heavenly banquet to come. What's the closest you have come to a heavenly banquet on earth? What made it that way? Consider planning a progressive meal, a traditional dinner party, a potluck, or a mystery dinner as a group.

❑ The parable of the Vineyard and the parable of the Wedding Banquet are stories with violent endings. Why? How do you make sense of the violence in our world today? How does the image of a violent God fit with the image of a God who is infinitely forgiving, embracing, and loving?

Pray first by reciting some of the wrathful images of God from the Bible. Then pray by reciting some of the loving images of God from the Bible. Pray for insight and understanding.

❑ In the parable of the Wedding Banquet, the king invites scads of people to join him in the feast in honor of his son, but the cost to each guest to stay at the party is high. Talk about your church's efforts to be inviting. What does it cost someone personally, financially, and theologically to be a member of your congregation?

❑ Make lemonade. There may be things about these parables that leave a sour taste in your mouth. What are they? Take two lemon slices. Taste one of the lemon slices. Experience its sourness. Then, confess one aspect of faith, the kingdom, or the parables that you consider "sour" or "bitter."

Take turns squeezing a lemon slice into a small container and telling how God could use even this bitterness for good. After each person who wishes has had a chance to speak, squeeze the remaining lemon slices, add sugar and water, and serve lemonade.

9. Bridesmaids and Talents: Signs of the Times

❑ Dan Otto Via says that Jesus tells two kinds of parables, tragic parables (those that emphasize strict justice or harsh judgment) and comic parables (those with grace-filled, happy endings). Talk about an incident in your life that was tragic or comic or both. What did you learn from it?

❑ Author Isak Dinesen says that "All sorrows can be borne if you put them into a story or tell a story about them." Can a story really make a difference in times of trouble? How? What stories have been a help to you in times of tragedy?

❑ Talents in the parables refer to an amount of money. But when we think of talents, we think of abilities or gifts. One of the best ways to figure out what God wants us to do with our life is to take a look at our abilities and assets. Check the areas where you feel you have some aptitude or talent:

__ listening/caring	__ working with old people
__ working with children	__ raising money
__ motivating/leading	__ hospitality
__ making people laugh	__ peacemaking
__ perseverance	__ getting others involved
__ problem solving	__ music/singing
__ teaching	__ working with children
__ prayer	__ evangelism

Let your group add two more things you are good at.

❑ The parable of the Talents encourages us to trust and take risks with the gifts that the Master gives. What risks have you taken in your life? How did they turn out? Is there a risk that you think God is inviting you to take now? Draw a picture of the best thing and the worst thing that could happen if you take this risk.

❏ Take a look at your personal budget or the budget of the church, and identify the areas that you would call "faithful but risky" investments. Where would God say to you, "Well done, good and faithful servant"? Where in your budget would God say, "Take a risk"?

10. The Sheep and the Goats

❏ Allow each person in the group to be the focus of group support, affirmations, encouragement, and praise. If you wish, combine your spoken affirmations with the sweet taste of pomegranate seeds (an edible symbol of resurrection—bursting forth from its hard shell like Christ bursting forth from the tomb). As group members offer you words of appreciation, eat a pomegranate seed. Savor the taste of the pomegranate seed as you enjoy the sweet taste of praise from other members of your group. At the end of the round, after each member has shared their words of praise, tell which words of affirmation tasted especially sweet.

❏ In the parable of the Sheep and Goats, list the six actions Jesus will use as the basis of judgment. How could the group do these six actions today? Do them now in whatever way you're able.

❏ The parable of the Sheep and the Goats lists some of "the least of these." Who else might you add to this list? Make a circle for prayer. In order around the circle, lift up someone who is the least of Jesus' family. Pause between each one for silent prayer.

❏ Have you ever been "one of the least of these" in any way (hungry, thirsty, a stranger, in need of clothing, sick, or imprisoned) and someone came to your aid? When have you reached out to people in these conditions?

❏   Give awards to the parables you have studied. Make up the
    categories: Most Unusual, Most Unexpected, Most Discom-
    forting, Favorite, R-rated for Violence, etc.

General Sharing and Prayer Resources

Forming a Covenant Group

Covenant Expectations

Covenant-making is significant throughout the biblical story. God
made covenants with Noah, Abraham, and Moses. Jeremiah speaks
about God making a covenant with the people, "written on the
heart." In the New Testament, Jesus is identified as the mediator
of the new covenant, and the early believers lived out of covenant
relationships. Throughout history people have lived in covenant
relationship with God and within community.

Christians today also covenant with God and make commit-
ments to each other. Such covenants help believers live out their
faith. God's empowerment comes to them as they gather in covenant communities to pray and study, share and receive, reflect
and act.

People of the Covenant is a program that is anchored in this
covenantal history of God's people. It is a network of covenantal
relationships. Denominations, districts or regions, congregations,
small groups, and individuals all make covenants. Covenant group
members commit themselves to the mission statement, seeking
to become more . . .

—biblically informed so they better understand the revelation
    of God;

—globally aware so they know themselves to be better con-
    nected with all of God's world;

—relationally sensitive to God, self, and others.

The Burlap Cross Symbol

The imperfections of the burlap cross, its rough texture and unre-
fined fabric, the interweaving of threads, the uniqueness of each
strand, are elements that are present within the covenant group.

The people in the groups are imperfect, unpolished, interrelated with each other, yet still unique beings.

The shape that this collection of imperfect threads creates is the cross, symbolizing for all Christians the resurrection and presence of Christ our Savior. A covenant group is something akin to this burlap cross. It unites common, ordinary people and sends them out again in all directions to be in the world.

A Litany of Commitment

All: *We are a people of the covenant; out of our commitment to Christ, we seek to become:*

Group 1:   more biblically informed so we understand better God's revelation;

Group 2:   more globally aware so we know ourselves connected with all of God's people;

Group 1:   more relationally sensitive to God, self, and others.

All: *We are a people of the covenant; we promise:*

Group 2:   to seek ways of living out and sharing our faith;

Group 1:   to participate actively in congregational life;

Group 2:   to be open to the leading of the Spirit in our lives.

All: *We are a people of the covenant; we commit ourselves:*

Group 1:   to attend each group meeting, so far as possible;

Group 2:   to prepare through Bible study, prayer, and action;

Group 1:   to share thoughts and feelings, as appropriate;

Group 2:   to encourage each other on our faith journeys.

All: *We are a people of the covenant.*

A Dancing Doxology

Carla De Solo has suggested some simple movements to give expression to the singing of the Doxology. Try them with your group.

Praise God from whom all blessings flow;
[*all extend hands over the table in blessing*]

Praise God all creatures here below;
[*all join hands*]
Praise God above ye heav'nly host;
[*raise hands, still joined, high in the air*]
Creator, Christ and Holy Ghost.
[*lower hands, still joined and bow deeply*]

A Prayer from Latin America.
"O God, for those who hunger give bread.
For those who have bread, give a hunger for justice."

Pretzel-baking as an act of prayer. Your time of prayer and study probably won't give you enough time to bake bread together, but you could make pretzels. Do this as an act of prayer and devotion. Listen to some meditative or inspirational music. Work together, as much as possible, without speaking.

The pretzel is a very ancient bakery item, which traditionally was eaten during Lent. It was made in the form of two arms crossed in prayer. The word *bracelae* (little arms) became *bretzel* (the pretzel) in German. These early Christians ate no dairy products in Lent, so the pretzel was made only of flour, salt, yeast, and water.

> Pretzels: 1 Tbsp. yeast
> $\frac{1}{2}$ cup warm water
> 1 tsp. honey
> 1 tsp. salt
> $1\frac{1}{3}$ cup flour

> Dissolve yeast in warm water. Add honey and salt. Add flour. Knead. Roll pieces to form pretzel shapes (or letters, symbols, animal shapes). Brush with beaten egg. Sprinkle with coarse salt. Bake 10 min. at 425 degrees. Serves 6. Note: For cheese pretzels, work $\frac{1}{4}$ cup grated cheese into dough.

For a closing prayer, offer your prayers in a circle as you clasp your neighbor's hand on either side (pretzel-like), arms and hands up, bent at the elbow.

Eating with Mindfulness. Psalm 34:8: "O taste and see that the Lord is good." Eat a meal together or give each group member a piece of fruit (orange, apple, banana). Invite the participants to experience the exercise of eating "mindfully." In silence, take several minutes to taste and experience the food. Use all of your senses—touch, sight, hearing, taste, smell.

Morning prayer. Encourage members of your group to start each day during the next week with prayer. In his book *Life Together*, Dietrich Bonhoeffer emphasizes the importance of how we begin the day: "For Christians the beginning of the day should not be burdened and oppressed with besetting concerns for the day's work. At the threshold of the new day stands the Lord who made it. All the darkness and distraction of the dreams of night retreat before the clear light of Jesus Christ and his wakening Word. All unrest, all impurity, all care and anxiety flee before him. Therefore, at the beginning of the day, let all distraction and empty talk be silenced and let the first thought and the first word belong to him to whom our whole life belongs: 'Awake thou that sleepest, and arise from the dead, and Christ shall give thee light' (Eph. 5:14)."

Take time to consider. Bernard of Clairvaux once said, "Worship is leaving time for consideration." Don't speak. Don't think. Don't act. Find a beautiful place (beneath the stars, beside a lake, beneath a mountain, in a desert, next to a tree, before a flower or a fire) and just *consider.* Repeat to yourselves the Bible verse: "Be still, and know that I am God" (Ps. 46:10).

Benedictine Meditation. St. Benedict popularized and refined a form of meditation that is divided into three parts: *lectio* (sacred reading), *meditatio* (meditation), and *oratio* (prayer). Start by quieting yourself in the presence of God. Breathe deeply. Relax. Then take up a book for sacred reading. The Psalms are a good place to start. Read until you light upon a word, a phrase, a sentence that touches your heart or captures your imagination. When you get to such a sentence, stop the *lectio.* Begin the *meditatio* by repeating this word, phrase, or sentence again and again. Through repetition, allow the words or image to sink into your heart and mind, to become part of you. After you have done this for a while, it is time to stop the meditation and start the prayer, the *oratio*. Pray spontaneously to God, in whose presence you sit, or just stay in loving silence before God. When you notice you are finding it hard to maintain the *oratio* without distraction, pick up the book and start the *lectio* again.

This is a helpful form of prayer for those who wish to begin moving from the head to the heart in prayer. It offers the head some participation in prayer, keeping it from becoming too distracted. At the same time, it gently takes the prayer away from rational discourse into simplicity and deep feelings.

Come, thou fount

Text: Robert Robinson, 1758
Music: American folk melody

Amazing grace

1 A - maz - ing grace! how sweet the sound, that
2 'Twas grace that taught my heart to fear, and
3 Through man - y dan - gers, toils, and snares, I
4 Yes, when this flesh and heart shall fail, and
5 The earth shall soon dis - solve like snow, the
6 When we've been there ten thou - sand years, bright

1 saved a wretch like me! I once was lost, but
2 grace my fears re - lieved. How pre - cious did that
3 have al - read - y come. 'Tis grace has brought me
4 mor - tal life shall cease, I shall poss - ess, with-
5 sun for - bear to shine; but God, who called me
6 shin - ing as the sun, we've no less days to

1 now am found, was blind, but now I see.
2 grace ap - pear the hour I first be - lieved!
3 safe thus far, and grace will lead me home.
4 in the vail, a life of joy and peace.
5 here be - low, will be for - ev - er mine.
6 sing God's praise than when we'd first be - gun.

Text: John Newton, 1779, 1790
Music: American folk melody, 1831

Christian, let your burning light

1 Chris - tian, let your burn - ing light shine on all with
2 As you jour - ney here be - low, shed a ray wher -
3 That your light may guide you through, bright - ly let it

lus - ter bright. Let your words and deeds be pure.
e'er you go. Find in this your pure de - light,
shine a - new. Keep up cour - age – nev - er fail

All for Christ you must en - dure. *Refrain* Chris - tian, let your light shine
let your light shine clear and bright.
till you're safe with - in the vail.

all a - long your way. You may guide a wan - d'rer to e - ter - nal day.

You may save from end - less night if you let your lamp burn bright.

Text and music: E. G. Coleman, 1898

Other Covenant Bible Studies

1 Corinthians: The Community Struggles (Inhauser) $5.95
Abundant Living: Wellness from a Biblical Perspective
   (Rosenberger) $4.95
Biblical Imagery for God (Bucher) $5.95
Covenant People (Heckman/Gibble) $5.95
Daniel (Ramirez) $5.95
Ephesians: Reconciled in Christ (Ritchey Martin) $5.95
Esther (Roop) $5.95
The Gospel of Mark (Ramirez) $5.95
Hymns and Songs of the Bible (Parrott) $5.95
In the Beginning (Kuroiwa) $5.95
James: Faith in Action (Young) $5.95
Jonah: God's Global Reach (Bowser) $4.95
The Life of David (Fourman) $4.95
The Lord's Prayer (Rosenberger) $4.95
Love and Justice (O'Diam) $4.95
Many Cultures, One in Christ (Garber) $5.95
Mystery and Glory in John's Gospel (Fry) $5.95
Paul's Prison Letters (Bynum) $5.95
Presence and Power (Dell) $4.95
The Prophecy of Amos and Hosea (Bucher) $5.95
Psalms (Bowman) $4.95
Real Families: From Patriarchs to Prime Time (Dubble) $5.95
Revelation: Hope for the World in Troubled Times (Lowery) $5.95
Sermon on the Mount (Bowman) $4.95
A Spirituality of Compassion: Studies in Luke (Finney/Martin) .. $5.95
When God Calls (Jessup) $5.95
Wisdom (Bowman) $5.95

To place an order, call Brethren Press toll-free Monday through Friday, 8 A.M. to 4 P.M., at **800-441-3712**, or fax an order to **800-667-8188** twenty-four hours a day. Shipping and handling will be added to each order. For a full description of each title, ask for a free catalog of these and other Brethren Press titles.

Visa and MasterCard accepted. Prices subject to change.

Brethren Press® • *faithQuest*® • 1451 Dundee Ave., Elgin, IL 60120-1694
800-441-3712 (orders) • 800-667-8188